THE ESSENCE OF

HUMAN–COMPUTER INTERACTION

THE ESSENCE OF COMPUTING SERIES

Published titles
The Essence of Program Design
The Essence of Discrete Mathematics
The Essence of Logic
The Essence of Programming Using C++
The Essence of Artificial Intelligence
The Essence of Databases
The Essence of Human–Computer Interaction

Forthcoming titles
The Essence of Z
The Essence of Compilers

THE ESSENCE OF

HUMAN–COMPUTER INTERACTION

Christine Faulkner

Prentice Hall

LONDON NEW YORK TORONTO SYDNEY TOKYO
SINGAPORE MADRID MEXICO CITY MUNICH PARIS

First published 1998 by
Prentice Hall Europe
Campus 400, Maylands Avenue
Hemel Hempstead
Hertfordshire, HP2 7EZ
A division of
Simon & Schuster International Group

Typeset in 10/12 pt Times
by Photoprint, Torquay

Printed and bound in Great Britain by
Ashford Colour Press Ltd, Gosport, Hampshire

Library of Congress Cataloging-in-Publication Data

Available from the publisher

British Library Cataloguing in Publication Data

A catalogue record for this book is available from
the British Library

ISBN 0-13-751975-3

---

2   3   4   5   02   01   00   99

For my parents.

Contents

Foreword

As the consulting editor for the Essence of Computing Series it is my role to encourage the production of well-focused, high-quality textbooks at prices which students can afford. Since most computing courses are modular in structure, we aim to produce books which will cover the essential material for a typical module.

I want to maintain a consistent style for the series so that whenever you pick up an Essence book you know what to expect. For example, each book contains important features such as end-of-chapter summaries and exercises and a glossary of terms, if appropriate. Of course, the quality of the series depends crucially on the skills of its authors and all the books are written by lecturers who have honed their material in the classroom. Each book in the series takes a pragmatic approach and emphasizes practical examples and case studies.

Our aim is that each book will become essential reading material for students attending core modules in computing. However, we expect students to want to go beyond the Essence books and so all books contain guidance on further reading and related work.

A well-constructed user interface is an essential component of any successful modern information system and this book provides an excellent foundation in the principles and practice of human–computer interaction (HCI). The material presented covers one of the essential building blocks of the computing curriculum and I am sure this will be a recommended textbook for many introductory modules in HCI. The book is written by an experienced teacher in a good, clear style, well illustrated with examples and practical guidelines. I enjoyed reading it and I feel that it should appeal to anybody wanting to find out about the basics of HCI.

RAY WELLAND
Department of Computing Science
University of Glasgow
(e-mail: ray@dcs.gla.ac.uk)

Acknowledgements

Grateful acknowledgement is made to the following sources for permission to reproduce material in this book previously published elsewhere. Every effort has been made to trace copyright holders, but if any have been inadvertently overlooked the publisher will be pleased to make the necessary arrangement at the first opportunity.

Figure 4.13: ©David Inman, 1997. Figure 4.17: ©South Bank University. Figure 8.8: ©Tom Boyd, 1997. Figure 9.4 ©Scottish Enterprise, 1996. Figure 9.6: ©Fintan Culwin, 1997. Figure 9.7: ©Nikolaos Vangalis. Figure 9.8: © Georgios Papatzanis, 1996.

Preface

This book is intended as an introductory text to human–computer interaction. The discipline is a vast one so in writing this book I have had to be selective about what I include or leave out. So far as is possible I have indicated in the further-reading sections areas that the reader might like to explore.

Each chapter starts with a brief overview and some end with a list of electronic resources. I have tried to be selective about the URLs because at the moment the Web is still young and URLs are notoriously changeable. There is a self test list with each chapter which is a glossary of any new terms. There is a complete glossary at the back of the book. For each chapter I have included suggested exercises which should encourage readers to develop their ideas. Readers will notice that occasionally there are what one reviewer called 'vignettes'. These are simply stories from my own or others' experiences which hopefully illustrate some of the ideas.

I have leaned rather heavily on my students past and present for the production of this text. The ideas have frequently been tried out on them and in some cases they have provided material.

A number of people helped directly and indirectly in the production of this book. Thank you to Georgios Papatzanis for the screen dumps of MINOAS and an example of an STD, Nikolaos Vangalis for the screen dumps of The Greek Gods and Glenn Elliott for the storyboards in Chapter 6 and to all the HCI students at SBU for stories and pictures for the book. Thanks also to Dave Inman at South Bank for permission to use his project web pages.

Thanks are due to Tom Boyd who provided material for Chapters 8 and 9 and took some of the photographs.

I should like to say a huge thank you to Fintan Culwin at South Bank who read the various drafts, kept me on schedule, made improvements, corrections, provided stories and various bits and pieces that appear throughout the book. But most of all, he was always there with advice and encouragement.

At Prentice Hall, I would like to thank Jackie Harbor for her support and encouragement, the series editor for the kind things he had to say about the draft he saw and an unknown reviewer whose comments, suggestions and often witty remarks made me view some of the text in quite a different light.

On a personal note, thanks are due to Anna Lucas for being such a good friend. She provided very practical help when it was needed even to arriving in my garden with a mug of coffee when I was proof-reading!

Finally, my grateful thanks to all those many people who have put up with me and the book, but especially to Rosie and Clarrie without whom I would have finished much sooner.

xristine@sbu.ac.uk

CHAPTER 1

An overview of human–computer interaction

Chapter overview

This chapter examines the background of human–computer interaction (HCI) and its role as a discipline. It looks at how HCI fits into the framework of software development.

1.1 The background to HCI

HCI is a term used to mean either human–computer interaction or human–computer interface. The former is the more common usage, though in the United States computer–human interaction (CHI) is sometimes used. It replaces the older and rather sexist man–machine interface or interaction (MMI), though in some ways MMI is to be preferred as it implies a breadth of study which is useful in the development of human–computer systems. It indicates that potentially computer interfaces of one sort or another will operate at all levels of our lives. The term human–machine interaction would certainly be an even better choice since it might serve as a reminder that computers are gradually infiltrating more and more of the machinery and equipment commonly used, and sometimes the interfaces and functionality of those everyday machines are hard for users to fathom. However, in this book the term HCI is used and is taken to mean human–computer interaction unless stated otherwise. Human–computer interaction is the study of the relationships which exist between human users and the computer systems they use in the performance of their various tasks.

HCI endeavours to provide an understanding of both the human user and the computer system, in an effort to make the interactions between the two easier and more satisfying. However, the emphasis should always be on the user. HCI is a discipline concerned with the optimisation of these two complex systems; computers are highly complex machines and human users are highly complex organisms. Human–computer interaction seeks to provide an understanding of how users function, the tasks they need to perform and the way in which a computer system needs to be structured to facilitate the easy carrying out of those tasks. The aim is to create computer applications that will make users more efficient than they would be if they performed their tasks with an equivalent manual system. This last point is very important, since all too often computerized applications are produced that do not make the user's task easier and more satisfying, nor do they save time.

To understand users it is necessary to understand the processes, capabilities and predilections that they might bring to the tasks they perform. This will involve an understanding and knowledge of such things as memory, vision, cognition, hearing, touch and motor skills. The computer system will need to be understood in terms of what it can do for users and how it might best communicate with them. Finally, the user's task has to be understood according to what it is, its relationship to other tasks and how it might best be accomplished using the computer system. Understanding all of these very complex parts is not easy. But hopefully, during the course of the following chapters, some of that complexity will become much more familiar and easier to comprehend.

Today it is necessary to add to these studies a wider understanding of the environment in which the user is active and performing tasks. Any good designer of a modern human–computer system should consider carefully the characteristics of the organization in which the tasks are performed. This requires an understanding of the sociology of the user's environment as users do not perform tasks in isolation nor is any task an isolated task. Thus, in studying human–computer interaction it is necessary to take a very broad approach and to consider as a matter of course socio-technical design and the solutions that this might give to the problems of designing systems for particular environments. Just as it is unrealistic to assume that all tasks are the same, so is it unrealistic to presume that all users are the same, or that all organizations act in a similar way. The task of HCI is to design for people, for tasks and for environments. If HCI is to be effective then it needs to consider all of these aspects in the design and development of human–computer systems. Later in the book the role of socio-technical design and its application for the realm of HCI will be examined.

In understanding the building blocks that can be used in the construction of human–computer systems, it is important to consider how the various potentials might be maximized. The interface has to play up to their strengths and compensate for their weaknesses. This is possible only if there is an understanding of the capabilities of each of those elements. To this end, anyone wishing to practise HCI needs to obtain a firm understanding of what the building blocks consist of, how they operate, and how they might interact with each other in a system. Thus, one of the primary roles of HCI is one of understanding and clarification.

1.2 The relationship of HCI to other disciplines

HCI is a multi-disciplined field. This means that it leans heavily upon other areas of expertise which, in turn, provide significant inputs to its operation and a framework for its practices. It needs to gain its inputs from many other associated areas of study because it has to understand both the computer system, the human user and the task the user is performing. The ability to develop a computer system will require an understanding of computer engineering, programming languages, input/output devices and so on. An understanding of the user will require an appreciation of human behaviour, of social interaction, of environment, attitudes, motivation, and so on. An understanding of task requires a means of identifying what is being done and why and in what type of environment.

Some readers may find Figure 1.1 rather frightening. They may fear that it means that they will need to know all about psychology, sociology, ergonomics and various other diverse and complicated subject areas before they can even approach the study of human–computer interaction. Of course, this would be impossible.

All of the subject areas mentioned above are suitable for study in their own right, so to take them on board at the same time as studying HCI would require an unacceptable effort on the part of an average person.

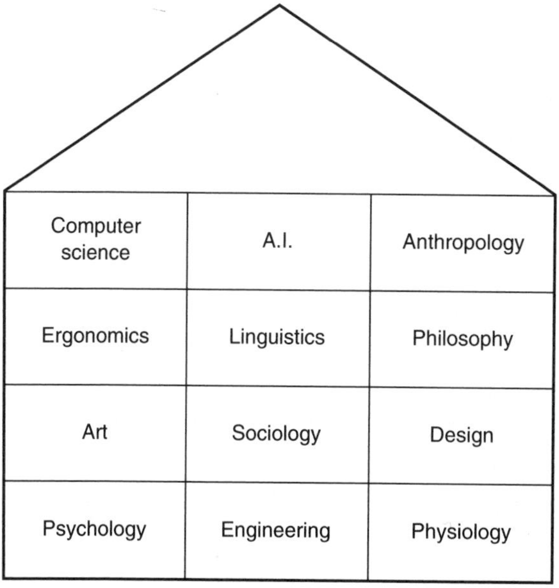

Computer science	A.I.	Anthropology
Ergonomics	Linguistics	Philosophy
Art	Sociology	Design
Psychology	Engineering	Physiology

Figure 1.1 *HCI and its building blocks*

But rather than being frightening, Figure 1.1 should be seen as a mark of HCI's strength. The vast inputs from other subjects make the study of HCI a source of inspiration and excitement. It means that experts in human–computer interaction can bring to HCI a wealth of knowledge obtained from very diverse sources.

In the past, HCI practitioners have come from many different fields, although many have a background in psychology. They have brought to the subject a vast range of skills, attitudes and abilities. However, in the past it has been very unlikely that any one person would have all of the expertise that was needed for the development of a human–computer system. Thus, HCI practitioners have often formed part of software development teams. Though they bring to the design of the interface considerable expertise and skill, they will also need to supplement this knowledge with sorties into different disciplines as and when this extra information is required. Figure 1.2 suggests some contributions that the various areas might make.

For example, it could be argued that the use of graphic artists might be a good idea to help with the design of screen displays or of icons since they would be accustomed to presenting information in an appropriate and eye

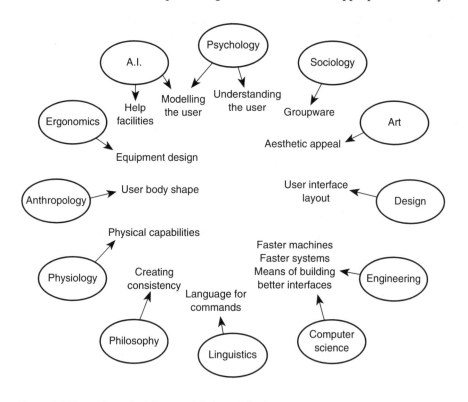

Figure 1.2 *The various disciplines and their contributions*

catching way. The student of HCI should be aware of the fact that it might be necessary to go much further afield than knowledge of the user, the task and computers in order to solve a particular problem for a particular system. Building a human–computer system might well involve seeking help from another expert who is not directly involved in the design or development of computer systems. It is the knowledge of what sort of information is needed in order to solve a particular problem that the study of human–computer interaction will hopefully provide. HCI still has much to learn from other subject areas as it is still a relatively young field of interest and it is still being defined.

All too often, a mention of HCI still gets the response 'What's that?' a sure sign of its youth. Certainly, the amount of input from each field varies according to the area of HCI being examined and probably it also depends on the person who is practising it. Some HCI practitioners view HCI as a branch of computer science and place the emphasis on the development of software. Others see it as a branch of psychology and spend their time studying people. Still others may see HCI as a branch of ergonomics and will place the emphasis on human capabilities. HCI courses and research can occur in computer studies or computer science departments, departments of psychology or departments of ergonomics. Depending on the subject area of the hosting discipline the nature of the focus for HCI will differ. Although a theoretical framework is necessary for the continued strength of the subject, theory alone is insufficient if it is not applied to the real world (Faulkner, 1995). Therefore, HCI needs a strong link with computing if it is to influence the software engineers of the future.

> In my own School of Computing, first year software development students study the problems of interface design as a matter of course. It is hoped that by exposing them early to the idea of user friendly design, they will see this as a natural part of the development of good software. When you are first learning how to program, the user seems to be the least of your worries, so it is a measure of the good work done by both the lecturers concerned with the delivery of that course and the students themselves that software is built that does attempt to consider the user. At the end of the day, HCI must deliver systems that are easier for the end user. The theory must be applied and must produce tangible results.

What remains true though is that all the time that HCI is involved in an attempt to solve the problem of how to make interaction with computers easier it will continue to draw upon material as and when it is needed. For example, if it was found that better interfaces could be built by using human abilities of taste then HCI would need to address more closely the problems of taste based interfaces. Many HCI practitioners would like to see HCI take on a larger role in the development of entire systems and to consider some of those aspects currently tackled by ergonomics too.

As systems develop it is likely that the areas of study will expand accordingly. HCI is not a discipline for those people who prefer their knowledge to be relatively static. HCI is constantly changing and evolving as the ability to build better systems develops. This tends to require a greater understanding of the way in which human beings operate with the systems they use. Furthermore, because HCI draws so heavily upon other areas of study, it has to readjust its own findings and practices as the body of knowledge in the other fields is added to or altered as part of the ongoing process of the development of ideas.

As well as being mutable, the material HCI has to deal with is often complex and contradictory because human beings are highly complex and some people would say contradictory too. To create better systems for people it is necessary to know about the person, the task being performed and the environment in which that task will be carried out. That way, good systems can be built that will actually fulfil the real needs of the user. These will be systems that will be used by the user because they do really help to perform the task required of them. In other words, it can be said that the aim of HCI is to know the user and to understand the task the user is trying to perform. If the designer of a computer application knows the user and also understands the task that this user is performing then there is a better chance of providing an appropriate system. Above all, if an understanding of user and task exists then the likelihood is that a system will be built that the user will adopt in preference to any other available tools that may or may not be computerized.

The coming chapters will examine both the end-user and the task being performed and the ways in which computerized systems can be built to make the performance of the task more efficient and more pleasant for the end user. In building the human–computer interface designers are helping to create a human–computer system which will be both efficient and satisfying to use. HCI practitioners are concerned with both these aspects of efficiency and user satisfaction, since a user who is satisfied with a system is likely to be far more efficient.

1.3 The importance of HCI

Today, computers are widely used by people who although they may be experts in their particular field, for example medicine, banking or flying aircraft, are not necessarily computer experts. In other words, they might know a great deal about the task they want to perform but nothing or very little, about the computer they use. It is important to recognize that the users may well be experts in their own right since an acknowledgement of this may well prevent the development of a system that talks down to them. It is necessary to accept that there is no real need for experts in other fields to become computer experts as well, any more than there is any need for people to be telephone engineers before they can use a telephone. It ought to be possible to produce computer systems that enable the user to perform the task without first acquiring a detailed knowledge of computer systems. The user's knowledge of the task ought to be quite sufficient to enable the successful completion of the task with the aid of a computer. If the human–computer system is properly built, the user will actually ignore it and will not notice that it is there. The very best systems and the very best interfaces will be overlooked entirely by the user. A good computer system, like a good pair of shoes, should feel natural, comfortable and fit without the user being aware of it.

Therefore, the aim of HCI should be to build computer applications that are jargon free and easy to use to the degree that all the user sees is the task and not the computer system at all! Although many people working with computers find them fascinating and rewarding, the same is not true of everyone. Therefore, designers of systems have to understand the centrality of the user's task above all else. It is the task that is important, not the means by which the task is done. Indeed, it could well be that the replacement computerized system creates a sense of loss in the user for the old manual system.

> I was once told by a graphic designer that although the computerized system he used was fast, efficient and relatively easy to use, he missed his compass, his pencils and rulers and the feel of the various pieces of equipment as he changed between them. He felt that he had lost some of his skills. As designers of computerized systems we need to take such sentiments seriously and to remember that the loss of tools and a perceived loss of skill are both stiff competition to our systems, however good we might think they are. Our computerized solution needs to make up for the fact that it does take away this close relationship between the craftsperson and the tools of the trade. If we fail to understand this then in some vital respect we fail to understand the user and the task being done.

It is the duty of systems designers to understand these feelings of the user and to make the system so easy and natural to use that the user is able to concentrate on the task alone. The loss of the manual system will not be mourned because the user is able to concentrate on the interesting and creative aspects of the task without worrying about incidental difficulties that may have got in the way with the manual system.

It is an economic fact of life that the cost of software is still relatively high and a competitive edge is more difficult to achieve for software companies wishing to sell their products. The interface to a system might just give it the desirable edge over that competition. Certainly, many users will judge software on the basis of the interface; after all the interface is the only part they see, and they will prefer one system over another because of its perceived relative ease. Once users have adopted a particular piece of software they are liable to remain with that product for all sorts of reasons, some of which are examined below:

1   The initial cost will make an immediate change to another system unlikely unless there is a pressing need for a change.
2   Upgrades to the application will hopefully build on the existing system and will not require a whole new way of thinking about the task so the user is unlikely to wish to swap to another product because of the retraining involved.
3   Software development houses usually offer reduced prices for upgrades, provided that an earlier version has been purchased. This will encourage customers to stay with their original choice of package.
4   The way in which the software encourages a user to think about the task will mean that the user comes to see that software as being intuitive.

Once organizations are using a particular piece of software, or computer system, it is difficult for them to extricate themselves, especially if they are a large organization and the software is used throughout that organization. This is referred to as being locked into a particular system. The cost of retraining an entire staff, both in terms of financial outlay and time, might well be prohibitive. Even where the cost in financial terms is not considerable, the task of retraining is not to be taken on lightly: people do not like to scrap skills they already have. The interface, therefore, must reduce the trauma of learning and maximize the ease of transition from the existing system to the new system.

Therefore, it can be said that the first impression the interface creates on the user continues to be of prime importance to those wishing to sell their products. The differences between two pieces of software might be minimal or non-existent in terms of performance and functionality, how quickly a task is performed and what tasks can be performed with the computer application. But the choice between the two products might seem to be profound to the end user who may well choose one rather than the other on the basis of how easy it appears to be to learn and to use.

It is expensive to train users of computer systems. The task of training involves both the learner and the trainer to be released from their usual tasks, although it is possible that the trainer's task is training! It has to be remembered that learners will be unable to be left alone to carry out the task until they are proficient in the use of the new system. It might be they require support for some time after the initial training has been completed, before they are sufficiently confident with the new system. The computer is just a tool and the employee is employed to perform a task. However, the tool is not important in itself and any necessary training is therefore a means to an end rather than an end in itself.

For all of the reasons discussed above, employees often resent having to spend time learning new systems and certainly employers would prefer that training was not necessary or, if it is absolutely essential, that it is kept to an absolute minimum. Employees who are either training or being trained are, as far as business is concerned, effectively unproductive. They might be learning something or teaching something but nothing tangible is actually produced. Therefore, it is true to say that a system that is easy and natural to use will save the organization money in the long run since it will require less training and less time spent in supporting the learner of the new system. Such a system is much more likely to be used than a system that requires more time spent on it both in terms of learning and in user support.

Lastly, as computer systems pervade more aspects of our daily lives, it is likely that legislation will gradually become wider in its application to software. There is already have some legislation that can be applied to software and its fitness for purpose. Eventually, software developers may be forced to face up to legal obligations to provide usable software. The HCI practitioner is ideally placed to take on board these considerations as part of the usability engineering process. Later chapters will examine some of the legal issues and usability engineering.

The aim of HCI is, therefore, to produce systems that are both natural and transparent to use. Above all, the aim of HCI should be to develop systems that do not involve the user in significant amounts of learning time or in significant amounts of learning effort. These systems should be effective, fun and safe to use.

1.4 The role of HCI in the development of software

Any new technology is too busy dealing with fundamental problems to cope with the niceties of how people might interact with that technology. The early car, the early aeroplane and the early computer were not considerate to their users simply because the technology was not far enough advanced to consider their users. People using these systems had to accommodate to the idiosyncrasies of that system. The driver of the early car, the pilot of the early plane and the user of the early computer all had to be experts in the fundamental operations of the systems they were using. Nowadays, that is no longer true and the designers of human–computer systems can no longer expect their users to accommodate to the system.

It is important to remember that the user is a person and not a human processor! Nor is the user a particularly unreliable component that is likely to cause the human–computer system to come to grief. The user is a person with a whole set of expectations and predilections. The success or otherwise of any system, computerized or not, may well depend on the co-operation of the end user. Where a system designer has the attitude that the user is an unreliable component this usually implies that the wrong things have been asked of the user. Quite obviously the user is unable to live up to the unreasonable expectations that the system designer has requested and errors are likely to occur. On the other hand, where a system has been designed to maximize the potential of the user and makes requests of the user which can reasonably be fulfilled then a proper human–computer system has been developed.

This positive attitude to the user leads to a process of user-centred design or in the language of ergonomics, fitting the task to the person. If the user is regarded as an unreliable component then a process of systems centred design has been followed or fitting the person to the task. When tasks and systems emerge from a process of fitting the person to the task then there is frequently an occurrence of 'human error' since the system design did not take into account the user's abilities. Such a process is analogous to having clothes made for you without providing measurements first. Pheasant (1991) suggests that by careful design much of so called human error could be avoided or at least minimized. However, he refers also to the consideration of working practices as another means of designing out human error. Sadly, HCI rarely, if ever, considers job design as part of the design process except when it is forced to examine the possible effects on the health of users caused by VDU use. No matter how good an interface is, if the design of the job is at fault the user will inevitably make mistakes.

The division of knowledge into neat little packets might be convenient for those wishing to obtain qualifications but, sadly, in the real world it can be a problem. The HCI expert should endeavour to absorb as much as possible from ergonomics so that in helping to implement computerized systems, the design of the task is considered. The problem is, of course, that systems are frequently designed away from users and therefore so generalized that no one knows for certain how the user will actually operate the system. The design of a spreadsheet, say, is worked on in complete isolation from all other tasks performed by the spreadsheet user. The result might be a wonderful spreadsheet and a joy to use, but this does not necessarily mean that the overall job of the individual has been made better or more pleasant, because the design is not in context.

Hopefully, it will become clearer during the course of this book just what might be deemed reasonable expectations of the user, and what must be considered unreasonable expectations. This knowledge will be gained only by a study of what people's performance levels are likely to be and that will inevitably involve an examination of human psychology and above all human information processing. These are all subjects for later chapters in the book.

1.5 Summary

- Human–computer interaction examines the relationships between humans and the computer systems they use.
- HCI is a young discipline and it still has much to learn. It is not a static area of study because it is evolving and concerns people.

- The material HCI looks at is changeable and complex and often contradictory: it aims to understand the user and the user's tasks.
- Computers are used today by all kinds of people doing all kinds of tasks. They do not expect to have to be computer experts.
- HCI is important in the design process since the computer interface is the first point of contact the user has with the system and the user will judge the system on the basis of the interface.
- HCI has a role to play in helping to define and ensure fitness for purpose.

1.6 Exercises

1 Consider each of the subject areas that have an input into HCI and consider what their relevance and application might be.
2 What differences might there be in the design of a system that places the emphasis on system requirements to that which places the emphasis on user requirements?

1.7 References

Faulkner, C. and Culwin, F. (1995) 'An integrated exercise in usability engineering'. In *Proceedings of the 3rd Annual Conference on the Teaching of Computing*.
Pheasant S. (1991) *Ergonomics, Work and Health*, London: Macmillan.

1.8 Further reading

Dix, A. *et al.* (1997) *Human–Computer Interaction*, 2nd edition, Hemel Hempstead: Prentice Hall.
This has as an excellent section on the computer and models of interaction and is highly readable. It makes a good, thorough follow-up text.

Norman, D. (1990) *The Design of Everyday Things*, New York: Doubleday.
This very popular book explains why it is that systems need to be usable. Norman gives many everyday examples of what happens when human beings are not considered in the design of objects and systems. This is an enjoyable book that examines the problems of users of systems and objects encountered in everyday life.

1.9 Electronic resources

The newsgroup comp.human-factors is well worth looking at for up-to-date discussion on HCI problems.

CHAPTER 2

The user's physical capabilities

Chapter overview

This chapter looks at user capabilities and suggests ways in which the design of computer systems can maximize on these capabilities.

2.1 Cognition

The term cognition is used to describe the interpretation of information from the outside world that is received through the senses. It is what enables the perception of objects and events and an interpretation of them to occur. This interpretation is extremely important to human beings as it could literally spell the difference between life and death. Simply seeing an object and hearing what sound it is making is not enough, this information has to be interpreted accurately and then acted upon (see Figure 2.1). The wrong interpretation of information could be fatal. This chapter examines some of the user's capabilities.

Figure 2.1 *Experiencing and acting upon the environment*

2.2 The senses

Information about the world is gathered through the various senses before interpretation can take (see Figure 2.2). These senses can be classified as follows:

- vision
- hearing
- taste
- smell
- touch

However, for most human beings, that is for those who do not have serious eye defects, the most important sense by far is that of vision – the ability to see. If you ask somebody what an unfamiliar object is like they will most probably describe it to you in terms of its visual appearance first and other characteristics such as its smell or its texture will be described later, if at all. When we want to know where a missing object is we ask if anyone has seen it. This reference to having seen it also implies knowledge of its location. So important is sight to us that our language is geared around it. The appearance of objects is very important to us. When we talk about something being aesthetically pleasing we mostly mean that it looks nice we do not usually mean that it smells nice or has a pleasant texture. If we meant that, we would enlarge upon our statement. In H. G. Wells's short story, *The Country of the Blind*, the sighted hero is struck by the patchy appearance of the blind inhabitants' houses when he sees them for the first time. To the blind inhabitants the visual appearance of their society is totally unimportant though, since other senses have been developed to replace the lost one. However, for most people visual aspects are perhaps the most important.

Thus sight, and then hearing, are the most important senses for the development of human–computer systems at the present time, though it might be that other capabilities are used in the development of computer systems in the future.

Vision   Hearing   Taste   Touch   Smell

Figure 2.2 *The senses*

2.3 Vision

When light enters the eye it has two main characteristics: brightness (intensity) and colour (wavelength). The range of objects seen by the eye are as a direct result of these two sources of information.

As children we are often told that the eye is like a camera. If you have no background in biology then that analogy is probably a good one to start with provided that you know how a camera works! Light enters the eye and triggers off sensitive cells at the back of the eye which form the **retina**. The retina is analogous to the film in the camera. The lens of the eye, like that of a camera, bends the light as it passes through it in order to make the image as clear as possible. This focusing is done by a series of muscles in the eye. The lens changes shape according to the proximity of the object; for close objects it is thickened and for distant objects it is flattened. This change in shape is called **accommodation** (see Figure 2.3). As we grow older the ability of the lens to change shape decreases both in the time it takes and the range. Hence, many older people are long sighted; that is they can see distant objects far more clearly than ones close to them.

The retina consists of a series of layers of nerve cells including a receptor layer which is made up of **rods** and **cones** (see Figure 2.4). There are about 130 million rods and 6 or 7 million cones. The rods are able to operate in conditions of bad light but they are unable to detect colour; the cones require good light in order to operate and can detect colour. This means, for example, that in the dark human beings are able to see shapes but are not able to detect their colours. The cones are concentrated at the front of the retina in an area called

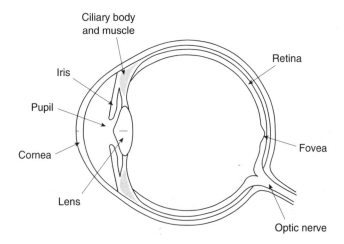

Figure 2.3 *Diagram of the eye*

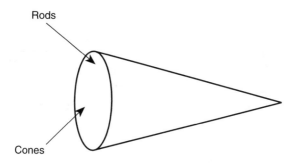

Figure 2.4 *The eye showing the relative positions of the rods and cones*

the **fovea**, and the rods at the sides. This means that colour detection is good when images are placed in front of the eye but not if an object is held to the side of a person. This can be important in the development of systems that involve large screens, or several screens or controls that intrude into the periphery of vision.

The retina responds to the light focused upon it by producing an electric impulse which is then passed to the brain for interpretation. This is done by passing data through the bipolar and ganglion cells. The receptors in the retina stimulate the bipolar cells and these in turn stimulate the ganglion cells. Messages are finally carried away from the eyeball via the optic nerve.

This is a gross simplification. It is important to remember that vision is not simply a product of the eye but involves interpretation by the brain as well. It is this interpretation which is responsible for some of the optical illusions which delight children so much. Obviously, in the development of human–computer systems it is important to avoid creating any confusing effects. This can occur with certain types of three-dimensional icons, for example, or can be caused by the misuse of colour. For example, a straight line can appear to be distorted if it is presented against a background of curving or radiating lines. Figure 2.5 shows some common optical illusions.

The following sections examine the most important terms which are used in relation to a discussion of vision.

Visual acuity and visual field

Human visual ability should enable a person to distinguish between separate projections on the retina. People should be able to do this clearly, without seeing a blurred object. This ability is called **visual acuity**. In normal daylight conditions visual acuity is best at the front of the eye – at the fovea. At this point, the receptors are at their most dense. In order to examine an object the

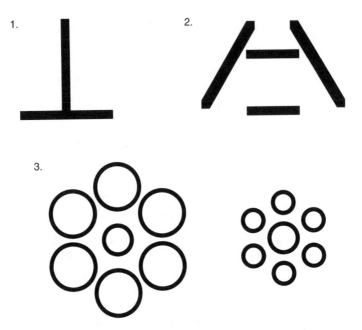

1. Upside down T – both lines are equal.   2. Ponzo – the horizontal lines are equal.
3. Tichener – both central circles are the same size.

Figure 2.5 *Optical illusions*

eyes will be moved until the object is in focus on the front of the retina. At the periphery of vision, a person may well be aware of the presence of an object without recognizing what it is. In order to see the object it is necessary to turn the head so that the front of the eyes can focus upon the object.

The **visual field** is the range in degrees discernible to the average human being. This varies according to whether or not the head remains stationary. If the eyes or the head are kept in the same position this will place severe constraints on the user of an interactive computer system. Usually, movement is allowed for and thus provides a range of about 100–120 degrees from the straight-ahead position. The visual field is important to the definition of the size of a display screen, the layout of the displays and of any controls. Too much movement of the head can cause discomfort and may also increase the chances of eye strain if re-focusing needs to occur (see Figure 2.6).

However, this does not mean that the user of a computerized system should sit motionless all day. This would lead to body fatigue at least. Systems need to be designed so that the minimum of head movement and eye movement is required but the user should not be asked to keep up that level of work and non-movement for long periods of time. Computerized systems should be built to

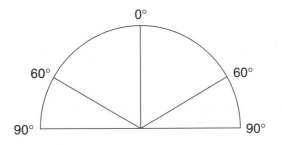

Figure 2.6 *The visual field*

minimize discomfort, but the overall work pattern of the individual should include movement and change of activity. Opticians have reported cases of young VDU users who suffer temporary short sightedness from working with VDUs all day. In designing human–computer systems it is important to understand that asking the user to focus at the same point all day without allowing the eyes to adjust to distance too, is creating an environment which may affect the well being of the user. These considerations will be examined in a later chapter.

Colour

Visible light is a small part of the electromagnetic spectrum. Our visual system is able to respond to wavelengths in the region of 400 to about 750 nanometers (1 nanometer = 1 millionth of a millimeter). This is called the visual spectrum. At 400 nm the visual system sees violet and 750 nm gives the sensation of red. Colour is classified according to **hue, brightness** and **saturation**.

Hue

Hue is roughly the same as what is normally meant when the word 'colour' is used in normal, everyday conversation. Hue is an aspect of chromatic colours (e.g. red and green). Achromatic colours (black, white and neutral grey) do not have hue. Hue varies according to wavelength. At about 465 nm unique blue is experienced (that is pure blue without any red or green in it). Unique green (that is pure green containing no blue or yellow) is experienced at about 500 nm. Unique yellow (that is yellow without any green or red) occupies the range at about 570 nm. Finally, unique red (that is red without blue or yellow) is produced by a mixture of wavelengths. It is called extraspectral because it is not produced by a single wavelength as in the case of the other colours mentioned above.

Obviously, the experience of these colours varies according to the individual perceiving them.

Brightness

Brightness is the subjective response to light, there is no real means of measuring absolute levels of brightness. Our perception of brightness is subjective and depends on our individual preferences and our individual physical make-up.

Where areas of dark and light meet it is possible to see strange effects – optical illusions. For example, in the Hermann Grid (see Figure 2.7) most people see black dots where the intersection of the white lines occurs and white dots where the intersection of the black lines occur. Try it on yourself and some other people.

Brightness varies amongst the chromatic and achromatic colours. This means that navy blue is perceived as being darker than light blue. White is brighter than black. Figure 2.8 shows some examples.

Saturation

Saturation refers to the extent to which the colour is a chromatic rather than an achromatic colour. The more black, white or grey that is mixed with the colour then the less saturated it becomes. When the colour is entirely grey, saturation is said to be zero.

Other considerations

Contrast is the relationship between the light emitted from an object and the light emitted from the background. Figure 2.9 shows the effect of four different

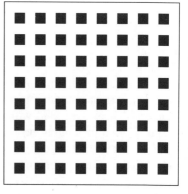

Figure 2.7 *The Hermann Grid*

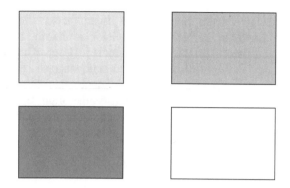

Figure 2.8 *Perceived brightness*

backgrounds with identical grey squares on them. The four grey squares appear lighter or darker according to the background. The lighter the background, the darker the central grey squares appear.

Luminance is the light reflected from the surface of an object and is measured in candelas per square metre. The greater the luminance of an object the greater the eye's ability to see detail. The diameter of the pupil decreases as the luminance of an object increases and this in turn increases the depth of focus. Also, the eye becomes more sensitive to flicker as the luminance of an object increases. The relative luminance of a screen will therefore partially dictate levels of flicker.

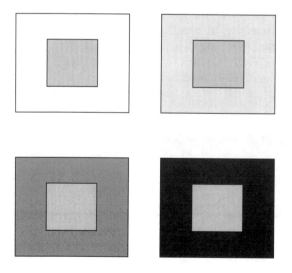

Figure 2.9 *Brightness contrast*

The brighter the screen the more likely a user is to see flicker. The eye is more sensitive to flicker at the periphery of vision so that the larger the screen the more likelihood there is of flicker being detected out of the corner of the eye. Flicker can be a cause of discomfort and annoyance. It can cause fatigue, headaches and feelings of nausea. There is evidence that although sometimes such effects are not commented upon by the user, the brain registers them with consequent undesirable results upon the user, such as headaches or even epileptic fits (LRD, 1991).

2.4 Design considerations

A person with normal colour vision is able to distinguish over 7 million different shades of colour. On the other hand, only eight to ten different colours can be identified accurately, without prior training, when examined in isolation by a person with normal colour vision. However, it has to be said that it would be unwise to produce systems which used all these colours at once for a number of reasons that are considered below.

Sensitivity to colour is not uniform across the whole field of vision. For example, the eye is not sensitive to colour at the periphery. It you ask someone to hold an object behind you and gradually bring it closer to your shoulder, if you keep your eyes ahead, you will eventually be aware of the presence of the object, but you will be unable to name its colour. Try it!

Accurate colour discrimination is only possible to ± 60° of the straight ahead position (the head and eyes are stationary) and the limit of colour awareness is about ± 90 degrees of the straight ahead position (see Figure 2.10). At the periphery of colour vision, the eye is least sensitive to red, green and yellow light and most sensitive to blue light. For this reason, blue makes a good background colour, especially where the screen is large.

At the front of the eye, where colour vision is at its best, the eye is most sensitive to red and yellow and is least sensitive to blue. Small blue objects tend to disappear on the screen, and this is especially true where the blue is

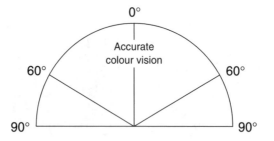

Figure 2.10 *Accurate colour vision*

pale. Small changes in shades of blue are difficult to distinguish but the eye is sensitive to small changes in red. In fact, the eye is sensitive to the differences between colours in various degrees and the discernment of colour differences is not uniform across the spectrum. Different colours also require re-focusing so spectrally extreme colours should not be placed together. The human eye would find it difficult to cope with red and blue together since this would require re-focusing which would inevitably be tiring. However, red, orange and yellow can all be viewed comfortably together.

Furthermore, the eye is not colour corrected so that warm colours (reds and yellows) are seen as coming towards the viewer and cold colours are seen as going away from the viewer. This could be used in the development of graphical user interfaces to suggest levels of activity.

A small percentage of people are colour blind – about 8 per cent of men and about 1 per cent of women. (For a woman to be colour blind both parents will need to be carrying the colour blindness gene.) For colour blind people, colour cues would be unreliable. It is evident that some people are unaware of their colour blindness and have adopted different means of identifying colours. This is probably associated with shade and depth of tone. The most common form of colour blindness is red–green but there are other rarer forms. A very small number of people have no colour vision at all.

Some people find the label 'colour blind' rather unpleasant and are unwilling to admit to being colour blind – an unfortunate term in that it implies a lack rather than a difference. Builders of interfaces have to be sensitive to this fact and should avoid colours which are liable to cause a problem.

> Colours that are likely to cause a problem implies more than one might at first realize. I once invigilated an examination where the students were given two answer books, one pale green and the other pale pink. They were told to answer section A in one colour and section B in the other. One student was confused and asked which was which. Other people in the room began to train him in colour identification as if he had never been taught which was which. The truth was that he was red–green colour-blind and unable to differentiate between the pink and the green books, the tones of each were so similar!

Incidentally, for those readers who wonder what red–green colour-blind people see instead of red and green then the answer is grey. A woman with red–green colour-blindness in one eye and normal colour vision in the other was able to describe what she saw with the colour-blind eye using the language of normal colour vision (Gleitman, 1992). Some colour-blind people have been fitted with contact lenses or spectacles to help 'correct' their colour vision (*Daily Mail*, 1996).

It has also to be remembered that classification of colour is both physically and culturally determined. Societies classify colour differently. Courtney (1986) took a large sample of Hong Kong Chinese and attempted to discover

Table 2.1 *The percentage of Hong Kong Chinese who associate particular concepts and colours*

Green	%	Red	%	Yellow	%	Black	%	White	%
Safe	62.2	Hot	31.1	Caution	44.8	Off	53.5	Cold	71.5
Go	44.7	Danger	64.7						
On	22.3	Stop	48.5						

Table 2.2 *The percentage of Americans who associate particular concepts and colours*

Green	%	Red	%	Yellow	%	Blue	%
Safe	61.4	Hot	94.5	Caution	81.1	Cold	96.1
Go	99.2	Danger	89.8			Off	31.5
		Stop	100				

the strength of association between eight colours and nine concepts. This data was compared with a study of Americans by Bergum and Bergum (1981). The differences between the two populations were substantial. Tables 2.1 and 2.2 show the results.

Courtney explained that for the Chinese, red is primarily associated with happiness and this association was so strong that it meant that it detracted from other possible associations. It is not possible, therefore, to assume that the 'correct' assumptions will be drawn from the use of a particular colour. Whether the user draws the conclusions the designer would wish will depend on the nature of the user's background.

Individuals vary in the levels of yellowing in the eye, making their perception of colour different. Furthermore, the colour detected by a user may depend on the level of brightness of the VDU screen so that asking the user to look for the bright yellow object might cause confusion if that user has the brightness control turned down. Such a user would see brownish objects.

Colour should therefore be seen as unreliable as a solitary cue and should be used as a means of reinforcement. Besides, short of visiting every user, you never know if they are using monochrome monitors and how the screen is adjusted for brightness!

The elasticity of the eye decreases with age. Also, the eye yellows with age making it even less susceptible to blue. Some people's eyes are naturally less elastic and more prone to yellowing so that sensitivity to brightness and to blue varies from individual to individual. It has to be remembered that older users may be less sensitive to blue and see colours as generally less bright. Additionally, older users usually require higher levels of luminance for their work area.

Certainly, the use of colour has to be considered with restraint and care. Although using colour can reduce the time taken to search, multi-coloured displays can actually increase search time (Oborne, 1995). It is probably true for most people that no colour is better than too much colour – the so called Las Vegas effect – though for children who like bright colours this might not be the case. For children, colour can catch the imagination and it may be possible to experiment much more with interfaces designed for the younger market.

Computer games are also less likely to need restraint in the use of colour, though again care is needed. One excellent computer game I am fond of manages to catch me out every time by displaying some information I would find useful in developing my strategies in blue, on blue and in shades that make it impossible for me to read.

It is probably true to say that the designers of systems should, however, experiment so far as colour is concerned and find out which combinations appear to best in testing. Hard and fast rules where human beings are concerned are always dangerous.

I remember viewing a system designed with a purple background and yellow text. This is not a good combination to work with in theory. I asked the designer why he had made such a design decision and received the reply that it showed up best when used on a black and white screen! There was one designer who knew the user and the platform she was using! I was later told by a partially sighted student that this too is the colour combination she preferred; it seems that she finds it much easier to see.

The aesthetic appearance of screen layout will also be a result of its visual impact. Because vision is a result of interpretation by the brain as well as information gathering by the eye, it is important to ensure that the layout adopted for the screen is visually pleasing and effective. This means making certain that the screen is not cluttered and that menu choices are arranged in a pleasing way. It is important to stick to the same sort of font, for example, as different types of font mixed together on a screen can lead to a jumbled effect. For example, this book is written using a particular font for the body of the text and the headings. It would be highly unreadable if every so often the font changed to something else and for no apparent reason.

There has been a lot of work carried out on font design. Originally, it was argued that serif fonts (see Figure 2.11) which have extra strokes on the letters were easier to read than sans serif, without serif, fonts which did not have those extra strokes (see Figure 2.12). The argument was that these extra strokes gave additional clues as to what each letter was. However, there have been suggestions recently that it is a matter of what you are accustomed to rather than the presence or not of those extra strokes. Nowadays, it is argued, because many more fonts are sans serif, readers are accustomed to seeing them and find

The quick brown fox jumps over the lazy dog.
The quick brown fox jumps over the lazy dog.
The quick brown fox jumps over the lazy dog.

Figure 2.11 *Serif fonts*

them just as easy to read as the serif fonts. Indeed, some people go even further and argue that sans serif fonts are easier to read than serif fonts. It may well be a case of opinion. But it is certainly true that it is bad practice to mix too many fonts. Figure 2.13 gives examples of various fonts.

However, the size of the screen will dictate, to a certain extent, how much information can be comfortably contained. Sometimes it might be necessary to restrict the number of things displayed at once. For example, main menu choices might be displayed and once a selection has been made a further list of sub menu choices can be shown. A cluttered screen is difficult to interpret because it is a lot for the eye and the brain to absorb. Too much clutter can be irritating because the user is bombarded with information which must be filtered in order to make reasonable choices about what the user wants to do. The design of the screen should endeavour to offer simplicity and should keep clutter to a minimum.

Also, it is important that items should be displayed according to their priority and they should occupy the same place on the screen, unless their priority changes. It is unwise to alter the position of an object unless there is a good reason to do so. Table 2.3 suggests appropriate times to attract attention visually.

The quick brown fox jumps over the lazy dog.
The quick brown fox jumps over the lazy dog.
The quick brown fox jumps over the lazy dog.

Figure 2.12 *Sans serif fonts*

The quick brown fox jumps over the lazy dog.
The quick brown fox jumps over the lazy dog.
The quick brown fox jumps over the lazy dog.

The quick brown fox jumps over the lazy dog.
The quick brown fox jumps over the lazy dog.

Figure 2.13 *A comparison between various fonts*

Table 2.3 *The use of the visual system for alerts*

Use visual feedback and visual means for attracting attention when:

The information is long and complex.
The information will be referred to later.
For alerts and warnings which do not need the user's immediate attention.
The user's aural system is already overburdened.
The user is not moving about.
A verbal response is not needed.
Illumination is good.

2.5 Hearing

For people with normal vision, hearing is the second most important sense after sight. For the blind, or the partially sighted, hearing or touch might be much more important than vision. In human–computer interaction, the second most important means of communication, for people with normal vision, is sound. Hearing, or audition, like touch is a response to pressure. However, it tells us about changes that occur at various distances away from us. These changes cause a displacement of air particles which then return to their original positions. Although each particle moves a tiny fraction this causes a series of successive pressure variations. When these sound waves reach the ears they cause a series of mechanical pressure changes which eventually trigger the auditory receptors. This causes responses in the brain and the sensation of hearing. Figure 2.14 shows a diagram of the ear.

Sound waves vary in: **amplitude**, the height of the wave crest; **wavelength**, the distance apart between each wave crest; and **frequency**, the number of

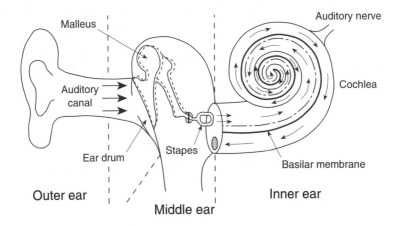

Figure 2.14 *Diagram of the ear*

waves per second. Amplitude and frequency are objective, physical dimensions. However, these are translated by the brain into loudness and pitch. A sound appears to be louder as its amplitude increases; pitch increases with the increase in frequency. Pitch is how high or how low a sound is.

Pitch and loudness

Frequency is measured in **hertz** (Hz). Most people can detect sound in the frequency range 20 to 20,000 Hz but the ability to detect the lower and upper ranges deteriorates with age and is also affected by health. Hearing is more sensitive in the range 1000 to 4000 Hz; this corresponds to the top two octaves of the piano keyboard.

The loudness of a sound is described in **decibels**. The threshold of hearing is defined as 0 decibels. Twenty decibels is a whisper and 50 to 70 decibels is normal conversation. Damage to the ear is likely to occur where the sound exceeds 140 decibels (see Table 2.4).

The ear is insensitive to frequency changes below 20 decibels. Human beings can distinguish sounds about 45 degrees apart. Sensitivity to frequency and loudness varies between individuals and can be different for the same person at different times. For example, hearing is frequently impaired if an individual has a cold.

Permanent hearing impairment affects about 10 per cent of the population and is not taken as seriously as sight defects, possibly because human beings tend to rely so much more on sight. It is only comparatively recently that hearing dogs have been introduced, whereas seeing dogs have been available for some time. Hearing impairment is very frequent amongst the elderly; this is especially true of sensitivity to the higher frequency sounds. People with hearing impairments are often quite loathe to admit to them and those provided with hearing aids are notoriously likely not to wear them, possibly because society is not as sympathetic and supportive as it might be.

Sound is used as a locator. Interestingly, the users of mobile phones seem to have difficulty recognizing whose phone is actually ringing and a mobile phone that rings on a train is likely to cause several mobile owners to check their phones. This is presumably because the positioning of each phone is not

Table 2.4 *Some sounds and their loudness*

Sound	Decibels
Spacecraft launching (from 150 feet)	180
Loud rock band	160
Thunder	120
Shouting	100
Conversation	50
Whisper	20
Threshold of hearing	0

Table 2.5 *The use of the sound system for alerts*

Use sound for feedback and attracting attention when:
The information is short and simple.
The information will not be referred to later.
For alerts and warnings when an immediate response is needed.
The visual system is already overburdened.
The user is moving about from place to place.
A verbal response is needed.
Poor illumination makes vision unreliable.

sufficiently distant. However, humans are normally adept at using sound as a means of locating things so that in some circumstances other tactics have to be employed. For example, scuba divers cannot locate the direction of a sound because sound waves travel much faster in water than in air so they are trained to look all around them when a hooter is sounded to alert them.

Sound is a good way of attracting attention since people respond more quickly to auditory signals than to visual signals.

Sound can be a source of annoyance and distraction. It is invasive as you cannot decide not to listen whereas you can decide not to look! All of us have been tormented by the 'non-personal' personal stereos! Use sparingly – like salt. Table 2.5 suggests some ways in which sound can be used and where it is most appropriate as a cue.

2.6 Touch – the haptic channel

The sense of touch is perhaps a little underrated so far as the development of human–computer systems is concerned. Touch is a very important sense for the blind or for those with severe eye impairments. It is useful in noisy (either visual or audio) environments where another channel is required to attract attention. For example, in one of the Bond films, James Bond's alarm watch woke him by tapping gently on the wrist! Tactile feedback is important in the use of the keyboard, for example. Users can complain about the 'feel' of a keyboard if it does not appear to be giving them adequate feedback. Certainly, typists using the early word processing packages frequently complained about the 'feel' of the keyboards. They said that keyboards were too spongy and they could not tell if the key had responded to the touch, required too heavy a touch or responded too readily so that several letters would appear after one keystroke. It was one of the major complaints made about early word processing systems. Incidentally, it was frequently the result of the wrong people doing testing on the system in that the computer system was tested and bought by the person in charge rather than being tested by the person who was going to use it (Bramer, 1988). This is a classic case of fitting the person to the task and failing to consult the real user of the system!

2.7 Taste and smell

Taste

The sense of taste provides information about what should or should not be eaten. It attempts to stop the living creatures from eating things that are poisonous. The receptors in this case are the taste buds which respond to chemicals that are dissolved in water. Most scientists working in the field of taste believe there are four basic tastes: bitter, salty, sour and sweet. It is thought that all other sensations of taste are produced by a combination of these tastes. On average, a human being has about 10,000 taste buds mostly on the tongue, although there are some in other regions of the mouth. Messages are passed from these receptors to the brain.

Smell

Smell or **olfaction** provides information about chemicals in the air. These excite receptors located at the top of the nasal cavity.

Smell is relatively unimportant to human beings although for animals like dogs it is of vital importance. Anyone with a dog will know that if you 'show' the dog something it will first sniff the object and then perhaps attempt to taste it. If, on the other hand you 'show' an object to human beings they will first look at it. If you want it to be smelt you would need to request that this be done.

It has to be said that smell probably has more effect upon us than we realize. Gleitman (1992) cites the example of studies done on a group of men and women who were asked to wear T-shirts for 24 hours. They were asked not to wash, use perfume or deodorants. After 24 hours each unwashed T-shirt was sealed in a plastic bag. Each subject was asked to sniff the contents of three of these bags. One bag contained her/his own T-shirt, a second contained a T-shirt worn by a man and the third a T-shirt worn by a woman. About 75 per cent of the subjects were able to identify their own T-shirt and could also say which had been worn by a man and which by a woman.

However, the senses of taste and smell are not used at present in human–computer systems as neither are highly developed in human beings although some people have developed either or both to extraordinary levels – for example wine tasters or experts in perfume. The sense of smell is affected by health and adaptation so olfactory displays are not widely used. Sanders and McCormick (1992) report of an unusual sign seen in a computer room which says:

'If the red light is blinking or you smell wintergreen, evacuate the building.'

2.8 Summary

Of the five senses, vision and hearing are the most important for human–computer systems at present, though touch is being used for some systems and has a part to play in input devices like keyboards.

The eye has two types of receptors: rods which are sensitive to light and cones which provide information about colour. The two receptors work together.

Perception is not simply a product of the senses; it involves interpretation by the brain.

Too many colours can be confusing for the user. It is best to stick to a few and to avoid colour combinations like red and green which may be confusing for colour-blind users.

Auditory alerts are responded to more quickly than visual ones. However, sound can be a source of annoyance so it is best to use it sparingly. It is difficult to avoid listening to noise without isolating the user and the sound from the rest of the environment.

Touch is important in the development of devices like keyboards. The speed at which a typist can type will be affected by the feel of the keyboard and how it responds to key presses.

Touch is a good way of getting the user's attention in an otherwise noisy environment.

Taste and smell are not well developed in people. As yet there are not real uses for either of these senses though both can evoke strong emotional responses.

2.9 Self test list

accommodation
amplitude
audition
brightness
cones
contrast
decibels
fovea
frequency
haptic channel
hertz
hue

Las Vegas effect
luminance
olfaction
retina
rods
saturation
visual acuity
visual field
wavelength

2.10 Exercises

1   You are involved in the development of a drawing package. What would be appropriate background colours? What would be appropriate for cursor position, lines and text? Explain your choice of colour.

2   You have been asked to help in the development of a system. The intention is to use colours to indicate the importance of items in a mailing system. Users can set their mail as being urgent, important, confidential, social, non-urgent. Suggest five suitable colours for the five levels of mail and give reasons for your choice.

3   If users were to be allowed to configure the colour of the mail system above for themselves, what if any, limitations would you place on them and why? Explain why it might be desirable for users to adopt the same colours and why it might be better for them to choose their own.

4   What are the major problems associated with the use of colour at the level of the interface? How can these be dealt with?

2.11 References

Bergum, B. O. and Bergum, J. E. (1981) 'Population stereotypes: an attempt to measure and define'. In *Proceedings of the Human Factors Society 25th Annual Meeting*, Santa Monica, CA: The Human Factors and Ergonomics Society.

Bramer, B. (1988) 'Problems of software portability with particular reference to engineering CAE/CAD systems'. *Computer Aided Engineering Journal*, September, 233–236.

Courtney, A. J. (1986) 'Chinese population stereotypes: colour association'. *Human Factors*, **28**, 97–99.

The Daily Mail 'New Specs Give Colour-Blind Boy a Brighter Future', July 6th 1996.

Gleitman, Henry (1992) *Basic Psychology*, 3rd edition, New York: Norton.

LRD (1991) *VDUs and Health and Safety*, London: LRD Publications.

Oborne, David J. (1995) *Ergonomics at Work*, 3rd edition, Chichester: Wiley.
Pheasant S. (1991) *Ergonomics, Work and Health*, London: Macmillan.
Sanders, M. and McCormick, E. (1992) *Human Factors in Engineering and Design*, New York: McGraw–Hill.

2.12 Further reading

Gleitman, Henry (1992) *Basic Psychology*, 3rd edition, New York: Norton.
This has sections on vision and perception. It is a good introduction to these senses. It has lots of examples and some interesting exercises.

Oborne, David J. (1995) *Ergonomics at Work*, 3rd edition, Chichester: Wiley.
This is interesting and useful for its thorough discussion of colour and text.

Rock, Irvin (ed.) (1990) *The Perceptual World*, New York: Freeman.
This a good introduction to sight. It is a series of readings taken from *Scientific American* and is entertaining and has some optical illusions to examine.

Salomon, Gitta (1990) 'New uses for colour'. In *The Art of Human Interface Design*, Laurel, B (ed.) Reading, MA: Addison–Wesley.
Has some good ideas about colour and advice on how to use it.

2.13 Electronic resources

Cornell Ergonomics Web
http://ergo.human.cornell.edu/

CHAPTER 3

The user's mental capabilities

Chapter overview

This chapter examines the user's mental capabilities and especially human memory. It provides a series of tests that the reader can try out to see how memory works. It also provides some guidelines for the development of systems.

3.1 Background

An understanding of human memory is arguably one of the most important aspects of human information processing (HIP) for those concerned with the development of human–computer systems. Modern day computer applications all too often operate as if users have amazing memories indeed. They expect the user to remember all sorts of apparently meaningless information. Even worse, one set of meaningless information learned for one particular application will more often than not be totally useless for another application which will necessitate remembering a different set of meaningless information. All of this increases the burden on our already overtaxed memories and leads to inefficiency caused through forgetting and perhaps to anxiety and stress at work.

> One of my colleagues has learned a phenomenal number of commands for the VMS/VAX. I once asked him how he remembered them all and he showed me a list in his filofax which he consulted if he forgot. I was appalled that it was necessary to remember so much apparently meaningless stuff. But he is so accustomed to the complexities of computer systems that he does not think there is anything bizarre about cramming his head with nonsense; it is just as well that memory is effectively infinite.

Like so much of human psychology, memory is a fascinating and highly complex subject. However, during the course of this chapter there will be time to do no more than acquire a very basic understanding of what human memory is and how it appears to operate. What is more important is that the student of

HCI develops a firm understanding of what the user can reasonably be expected to remember when working with a computer system. It is of the utmost importance that unnecessary burdens are not placed on the user's memory. But at the same time, the intention is not to create a system that does not maximize the potential of both the human user and the computer system. The object of this chapter is, then, to provide an understanding of the strengths and weaknesses of human memory in order that we might avoid overtaxing it.

During the course of this section there are a number of experiments that you might like to do. However, you may prefer to read through to the end of the chapter and then try out the experiments on some other people. The experiments are hardly scientific but the aim is not to build on the body of psychological knowledge but to give you some idea of the sort of experiments that have been done on memory and also to give you a chance to look at the way in which your own memory works. It is very important to understand that there is no such thing as the average memory. There is no such thing as doing well or badly in the tests. It ought to be an opportunity to reflect.

Before you go any further, there is time for a very short experiment. Read the series of letters that follow and then try to memorize them. You need to learn them just as they appear on the page, in the exact order and position. Spend a couple of minutes learning them and then, when you are ready, continue reading through the rest of this chapter.

gnihsilbup

potksed

3.2 An overview of memory

Human memory probably consists of a series of connected systems. There is not general agreement on the form it takes, but one of the most useful descriptions for the purpose of human–computer interaction consists of recognising three types of memory. These are:

- long term memory
- working memory
- sensory memory

Long term memory is where memories are stored. Working memory is effectively where conscious thought processes operate. Sensory memory is the area of memory which copes with inputs from the senses (see Figure 3.1). Each of these will now be considered in more detail.

Working memory or short term memory

There is much debate about the nature of memory, whether it consists of separate systems or a unified system, operating in different ways according to

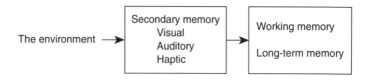

Figure 3.1 *Types of memory*

its needs and purpose. In the past, psychologists have identified short term memory (STM) and long term memory (LTM). STM was seen as an area of memory that was able to hold limited information for a short time and this information would fade or be forgotten if it was not constantly refreshed. Today, the work of psychologists like Alan Baddeley has led to the development of an alternative view of memory. Briefly, Baddeley suggests that memory consists of LTM and something he calls working memory (WM) (Baddeley, 1990). He argues that in effect STM exhibited itself in memory experiments and is an aspect of WM, and its limitations. For the purposes of HCI, although it is convenient to think of separate types of memory it is probably easier to view memory as a single entity that exhibits different aspects of itself depending on the circumstances under which it is operating. For example, a car is still a car if it is travelling at high or low speeds. At high speeds it may be less stable but will travel faster. At low speeds it is more stable, has more ability to pull but needs more time to cover distances. Memory can be seen in the same way, with working and long term memory being aspects of the same organization but performing different functions and having different strengths and weaknesses. Both aspects are part of the same system.

The area of conscious memory where current processing takes place has been labelled working memory by some psychologists in an effort to illustrate a difference between it and long term memory where concepts are 'stored'. It is sufficient for the purposes of understanding the user of a computer system to say that working memory acts as a place where information can be worked on by the conscious thought processes. It can be fed by the memories stored in LTM or those provided by the various sensory receptors. It is limited and it is this limitation that affects the type of computer interface that might be developed for particular users.

What was previously labelled short term memory (STM) can therefore be seen as an aspect of memory when it is in working mode. STM and therefore WM are limited in capacity whereas LTM is not. This limitation of STM has in the past been taken to be about seven, plus or minus two, pieces of information; this has come to be known as the magic number 7 plus or minus 2 after George Miller's seminal paper (Miller, 1956). But this will be examined in more detail later on.

Long term memory

Long term memory (LTM) is an area of memory where information is stored and can be retrieved over very long periods of time. To all intents and purposes, long term memory (LTM) is infinite. In other words, it is very unlikely that an individual will be able to fill up their memory during a life time. However, memory traces do appear to become less accessible and humans do appear to forget things. Freud believed that information is never really lost from long term memory at all but it becomes less and less accessible. It would be a nice argument to decide that if the memory trace to a particular concept was very faint, effectively that memory had disappeared. Freud believed that under the right circumstances the material could be retrieved but as there is little or no control over this process the state of forgetting can be viewed as sometimes perhaps quite permanent. The inability to recall information as desired, what is termed forgetting, could be viewed as very long retrieval times. This can be borne out by the way that when you try to remember something it can suddenly come to mind many days later and perhaps when you think that you have stopped thinking about it altogether. Why people forget is not really understood either though sometimes there appears to be a block on that particular memory. Freud (1901) believed that forgetting was often a quite deliberate action on the part of the individual though of course it was unconscious.

Electrical stimulation of various parts of the brain have caused those taking part in this operation to say that various memories have sprung to mind when the stimulation took place; however, the data available is inconclusive. Indeed, today there is much argument about how memories are stored. It has been suggested that they are not stored in places at all, as we might store letters in a drawer or sheets in an airing cupboard but are diffused through every part of the brain. It might be convenient to think of memories as being stored like data in an array with each packet consisting of a fraction of the entire memory and a pointer to where the next element is stored. However, for the purposes of HCI it is sufficient to talk about storage of memories but it is sensible to remember that the understanding of the human brain is still far from complete. It may well be the case that it is necessary to alter the way in which we think about aspects of human memory in the future, if new material comes to hand.

There is no control over the way in which material will be stored and related and there is not complete control over what will be remembered in long term memory since we can often remember events that we would prefer to forget and forget things that we would rather like to be able to recall (Freud, 1901). The psychology of this is actually well beyond the scope of this book and for the time being is not examined by HCI. However, it is important to remember that all of these representations of human behaviour remain very simplistic. Although it is possible to design systems to be easy to use and easy to learn it is not possible to account for the individual who forgets because of a psychological block caused by specific psychological makeup. This inability may need to be considered when it comes to testing a system.

> For example, one of my colleagues told me that he often forgets to press the return key after sending a document to the printer. I remarked that this was unusual as he was an expert user and accustomed to hitting return in order to confirm decisions. He thought about this for a while then admitted that he disliked going all the way down a flight of stairs to collect the print out. Unfortunately, there is little we could do about that.

Items from LTM have to be retrieved and brought into working memory before they can be used; this is the process of **activation** and, obviously, it takes time. The equivalent parallel in computing terms would be the difference between an array and a file. The array holds less information but is held in volatile memory so the time required for processing it is quicker. On the other hand, a file can hold vast amounts of information but that information has to be read into volatile memory before it can be used and this requires more processing time. LTM and working memory are like that. Items in working memory can be processed more quickly than information which has first to be retrieved from LTM. Thus any system that requires recall from long term memory will slow down the activity of the user.

Sensory memory

Sensory memory is an area of conscious memory that deals with information from the senses, that is, from the ears, nose, eyes, tongue and haptic channel. There appears to be a separate store for each of these as information received from the senses can be 'replayed' or evoked at will and seems to be separate from working memory. You might be aware of the smell of something burning before you actually process this information. Some sensory memories appear to be more durable and effective than others. For example, the aural memory is better than the visual memory in this respect.

Memory for taste and for smell is perhaps even more elusive though it is clear that individuals can vary a great deal and some people, for example, perfumiers, have developed their senses of smell to a remarkable degree and can identify the various components to a particular smell. This might seem surprising at first but if you consider an animal like a dog, for instance, it is less surprising. A dog's sense of smell is vastly superior to our own. A dog will remember a person by recalling that individual's smell. That information might be stored for years in much the same way as human beings might remember someone's face. What is certainly true for most people is that smells can evoke strong memories and some smells and tastes can be recalled given suitable stimulus. As yet, computer systems do not use smell or taste since it is not yet obvious how these might be used. However, virtual reality may eventually need to consider all the senses and use them in order to create the atmosphere of a

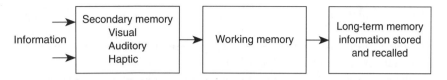

Figure 3.2 *Human information processing – a model of memory*

real experience. Furthermore, it has to be noted that the demand made upon human eyesight is considerable, and often to the detriment of all else. It might be that in the future it is desirable to reduce the load on the visual system and to increase the load elsewhere.

Episodic memory and semantic memory

Besides the existence of long term memory, working memory and sensory memory a useful distinction can be made between the types of memories that a human being might have. The following can be identified, for example: episodic memory and semantic memory.

Episodic memory involves memory of events – for example, what you had for dinner, or where you went on Saturday.
Semantic memory is knowledge about the world – for example, what different words mean, how many inches there are in a foot.

This provides an initial background to the workings of human memory. It is by no means complete and is simplified for the sake of clarity but should prove to be sufficient for the moment.

3.3 Memory in action

It is now possible to consider the role of memory in human information processing, in far more detail. For example, working memory has a consider-able role to play in both language understanding and calculation. In both these cases, there is a need to hold ideas in your head while the process of interpretation of the words or the calculation is carried out. For example, to understand a sentence you need to remember the beginning while you read through, or listen to, the end. If you could not do that, you would be unable to recall the subject of the sentence. There are people with brain damage who find this task either difficult or impossible and it is partially from study of such people that our understanding of memory has advanced. In the process of sentence understanding, working memory must play a part otherwise you would never manage to make sense of the world (Baddeley, 1994). Once the material has been dealt with it can be stored or dispensed with as necessary. Some ideas will be effectively lost but others will be recalled and might be replayed through thinking about them or repeating them to other people.

On the other hand, sensory memory is involved in the processing of information received through the senses. For example, when you watch a film you see a continuous moving scene although actually you are shown a series of still pictures interspersed with periods of darkness. The visual system stores the information from one frame (a still picture) until the arrival of the next one. These are then put together by the brain in a way that makes them seem like a continuous scene. This is because our understanding of the world tells us that people do not suddenly appear in one place or another; they have to move from one area to the next.

You can try this out for yourself on bonfire night by getting someone to make circular movements with a sparkler; you will notice that you can see a circle because the eye remembers the trace and the brain turns this into a continuous picture. You could produce a similar effect with a torch, if bonfire night is too far away. Similarly, it is possible to play back words which are heard. If someone says something and you realise you have not understood it, you can 'play back' what they said in much the same way that you can play back a tape recording. The sensory memory for the ear appears to be rather more durable than that for the visual system since from experiments with memory it is known that a list that is read out will give fewer errors in recall than would be produced by the examination of a written list. This is possibly because the information is coded in two different ways.

> As a colleague and I passed an office one Friday evening, we heard Mozart's *Requiem*, albeit a bit loudly if you dislike Mozart. Someone shouted something and my colleague repeated, 'Turn that vowell down', and then after a moment's thought 'Turn that row down.' He added that he had 'run it through again' to make sense.

3.4 Memory experiments

Many experiments have taken place on memory and these have allowed a picture of human memory to be built up. All of the following can be considered when studying human memory. Where possible you should try out the experiments for yourself. Although your findings cannot be seen as conclusive they will help you to understand how your memory works.

The digit span

In considering memory it would be advisable to look at some aspects that have emerged from experiments carried out in the last hundred years or so. The question of the capacity of short term memory (STM) was studied by a London school teacher, J. Jacobs, in 1887. His experiments, carried out on his pupils, led him to devise a technique which he called the **digit span**. This had quite a profound effect upon the type of experimentation carried out on memory and its

```
4 5 7 9
3 8 2 5
6 5 1 4
8 3 1 9 2
6 8 2 5 9
5 4 2 8 1
9 1 3 8 2 5
6 4 8 3 7 1
5 9 6 3 8 2
7 9 5 8 4 2 3
5 3 1 6 8 4 2
5 2 7 1 4 6 8
8 6 9 5 1 3 7 2
5 1 7 3 9 8 2 6
3 1 5 9 8 2 4 7
8 2 7 4 1 9 4 3 5
7 8 3 1 6 4 9 5 2
6 1 5 9 3 3 8 2 6
9 1 5 2 3 3 8 1 6 2
7 1 5 7 9 9 6 1 9 3
3 8 2 9 6 6 7 3 1 8
```

Figure 3.3 *The digit span*

legacy can still be seen in modern memory experimentation. In fact, society tends to classify people as having good or bad memories based on the results of memory tests like the ones Jacobs performed. Those people with large digit spans are classified as having good memories.

The digit span is determined as follows. The subject is presented with a series of digits and is asked to repeat them back in the same order. The number of digits is gradually increased until finally the subject always fails to recall the list accurately. The sequence length at which the subject is right half the time is the digit span.

You can try this for yourself. Make a note of when you get the sequence wrong and from this you can derive your digit span. A set of numbers for you to try this on is provided in Figure 3.3.

Chunking

George Miller's experiments showed that the capacity of short term memory is 7 plus or minus 2 chunks of information. More can be remembered if the items can be chunked. This means that pieces of information are grouped together so that they form one item to be remembered. Miller referred to this as the magical number 7 plus or minus 2 (Miller, 1956).

Obviously, this has implications for the designer of a computer system. It means, for example, that it would be advisable to try not to present more than 7 plus or minus 2 items to the user, for the user to recall. Also, passwords of more than 5–9 characters would be difficult for most people to remember unless chunking is possible. These chunks are not always obvious or predictable so that what is easy for one person is difficult for another. It is important not to assume that because one person finds a task easy another will be able to perform the task just as easily. Memory capacity varies from person to person and even within the individual there are variations. Some people seem to have good memories for faces, or for numbers and so on.

Chunking means the grouping together of information into sections that make sense to the individual and are seen as entities by that individual. This does not necessarily mean that the chunks will be the same for everyone although this will undoubtedly sometimes be the case. For example, the following sequence of numbers might be quite difficult to recall if you treated them as an entity:

051594737

However, if you treated them as a series of three chunks you would find it much easier to remember (Baddeley, 1990):

051 - 594 - 737

Most of us can easily remember telephone numbers of that length or perhaps even longer.

Similarly, you would find it difficult to remember the letters:

G G N N T I H I A U

But you would find it much easier to recall the following:

H U N G A T I N G

The reason that HUNGATING is easier to recall than GGNNTIHIAU is that the letters of the former can be divided into two bits HUN and GATING. If you were asked to remember a real word you would find it even easier because the material would make sense and is therefore in the form of one chunk of information. A sentence consisting of several words would likewise be seen as one piece of information because of chunking and can easily be recalled. All of us have been able to repeat something said to us earlier; whereas nonsense words of a similar length would be much harder to remember. For example, it is easier to remember:

'But pleasures are like poppies spread:
You seize the flow'r, its bloom is shed;'
from *Tam O' Shanter* by Robert Burns

than it is to remember:

> 'Twas brillig, and the slithy toves
> Did gyre and gimble in the wabe:'
>
> from *Jaberwocky* by Lewis Carroll

Primacy and recency effects

From experimentation on memory it is possible to make some generalizations about the way in which human memory works. Table 3.1 shows several sets of words. Read through each list in turn once at a steady rate and then try to recall as many as you can by writing them down as soon as you have reached the end of the list. Do not spend too long over it, just a few minutes.

Recalling lists in any order is known as **free recall** and it is easier than recalling lists in order. In free recall exercises there is a tendency for the first one or two words to be remembered well; this is called the **primacy effect**. It is suggested that the first words are rehearsed several times and the subject effectively learns them, or they enter long term memory. Next, the words in the middle will be less well remembered while the words at the end will generally be well remembered; this is called the **recency effect**. The words at the end are remembered because they are still present in working memory or even in the auditory loop if they have been heard. Rare words are less likely to be remembered than common words. And words that create a strong image (like elephant) are well remembered since they are probably coded both as a word and as a visual image. When this double coding occurs the concept is much more likely to be recalled.

Table 3.1 *Memory test*

List 1	List 2	List 3	List 4
barrier	babies	mug	file
firearms	sofa	post-card	heart
scarf	lobby	table-lamp	scarecrow
newspaper	clock	chinchilla	stylus
sea-shell	polish	eraser	maggot
tomato	lintels	hat	rug
apologies	dog	tissues	flea
table	dolls-house	vase	ball-pen
plant	oasis	pot-pourri	jamboree
chemist	festival	pencil	Neptune
identity	gnat	fire-place	magnum
percolator	curtains	candle	paper-clip
saucer	income	wine	typist
tiles	precinct	rocking-chair	subway
directory	argument	raisin	accident
recall	recall	recall	recall

I once used this idea on a group of students. Amazingly, the number of students who remembered the word 'elephant' was very impressive indeed. I explained in some detail how strong images were easy to recall. I went on at great length about the appeal elephants had for us when we were children, and so on and so forth. I concluded that we needed to use this fact in the design of systems. At this stage, one of my students pointed out that I was wearing my usual elephant earrings and that had provided them with a cue! It is all too easy to overlook the obvious where human beings are concerned. Be warned!

The way in which information can be chunked can also aid the storage and retrieval of words. For example, at the start of this chapter you learned a series of letters – try to recall them now. You may not have noticed that it read 'desk top publishing' backwards! If you did, that would have made it easier to remember because it would have been chunked as a unit. However, if you did not then you may have relied upon mnemonics, things to help you remember, such as making up stories, family names, in order to help you remember.

There is time for another experiment before you move on. This time before you recall the list, perform the calculations after each list. Do the sums in your head, then recall the list just as you did before. A table of three lists and sums can be found in Table 3.2.

You probably did less well this time. When subjects are given lists and then asked to perform calculations, or any other activity, before they are allowed to recall, the other activity interferes with rehearsal of the material and leads to a decay of the memory of words at the end of the list. In other words, the words at the start of the list would be recalled but the rest of the list would be less well remembered. The primacy effect would still operate – the first few words would generally be well remembered. However, the recency effect would be destroyed by the task of having to do the calculations. Try it on someone else and see.

Closure

When you look up a number in the telephone directory and rehearse it before dialling, once dialling is complete there is a feeling of relief. This is called **closure** and it is very important to remember this when constructing interactive computer systems. For example, when you log on a computer system if you are successful you are greeted with the welcome message. You know that you are ready to proceed to the next stage. Human beings like to know when a task has been accomplished since it means that they are free to move on to the next stage and forget about the task they have just done. You may have felt the same sense of relief when you no longer had to remember the series of letters at the start of the chapter. All the time you were trying not to forget you probably felt as if you were under tension. It is difficult to concentrate fully on another task

Table 3.2 *Memory test with calculations*

List 1	List 2	List 3
aubergine	rescue	angora
chickenpox	gravestone	stable
elephant	flower	greetings
telephone	fountain	hanging-basket
pendant	statue	course
egg	fool	purse
melancholy	aphid	caterpillar
cheese	surprise	jumper
mug	printer	biscuit
nymph	cenotaph	baton
dinghy	dog basket	gnome
tray	magnet	cook
mole	lawn	chocolate
tram	pram	parcel
macabre	sandwich	teapot
6	7	1
+5	+2	+6
+3	+5	−4
+8	−3	+9
−5	−2	−2
−1	+9	+8
+7	+4	+9
−3	−6	+6
+9	+8	−3
recall	recall	recall

when you are desperately trying to remember something which is not particularly easy to remember.

It is important to build closure into systems since this acts as a means of allowing processes to be grouped or chunked in memory. The process will later become a whole chunk for the expert user, this will be examined later when we look at the differences between novices and experts. The act of providing closure will also be a means of giving feedback to the novice user and this will aid the learning processes and reduce the burden on memory.

Maximizing memory

There is evidence that information that is coded in more than one way, is easier to remember than information that is coded in one way. For example, if a subject is presented with a series of pictures, these should be easier to recall than the corresponding word. There is much evidence to support the consideration that human beings are able to recall pictures better than they can recall words. This tendency is used as an argument for the development of direct manipulation or iconic interfaces. This subject will be examined in more detail later.

It is important that the user feels comfortable when using a system. In states of arousal – fear, anguish, elation, or any other extreme emotion, human beings are less likely to remember things. Experiments performed by Loftus (1979) have shown that eye witness accounts of crimes can be highly unreliable. This is because the witness is often distracted by the fact of violence or is not able to retrieve the information at will.

> A close friend of mine once unwittingly witnessed a robbery. She had a few moments before passed by an empty car with the engine running. She noticed the make of the car because she had once owned one just like it. She noticed the registration number since it reminded her or a game she used to play with her father when she was a child. She also passed the person who had committed the crime but she thought that he was someone in a hurry, carrying a bag of sweets. When the police asked for witnesses she was able to give the entire registration number, the make of the car and its colour. She had not consciously memorized that number. The police were at first sceptical but later found her to be quite correct. She was asked also to give a description of the man she had seen. She surprised the police and many of her friends by not being able to say anything at all about him, except that he was a man. She insisted she couldn't describe him beyond the fact he was carrying a paper bag. Later she was told that the man had a very bushy beard. My friend had not remembered or had failed to notice!

A user interface must encourage a relaxed attitude since users are more likely to succeed with the system if they are not under stress. However, relaxed does not imply that the user is likely to fall asleep! Sadly, there is no evidence to support the idea that learning can take place during sleep and the user has to be awake and alert (Baddeley, 1994). You cannot use sleep learning techniques as a means of revising for those human–computer interaction examinations. Experimentation on sleep learning tends to suggest that the 'learner' can recall only those snippets of information that they managed to hear before they fell asleep; they do not learn during sleep.

Baddeley (1994) has suggested from his experiments with scuba divers that people are more likely to recall information accurately if they are able to recall it in the same situation it was learned in. Divers found it easier to recall items they had learned under water when they were under water and things learned on land were better recalled on land. This also applies to physical states. Subjects asked to recall where they had left items when they were intoxicated were much more likely to remember their location when they were next drunk than when they were sober. This would seem to suggest that learning how to use a system might best be done in the same environment/state as that in which the system is to be used. This is a point worth bearing in mind when you come to the testing and evaluation of a system. It is far better to train users and evaluate a system in the environment it will operate in.

Anderson suggests that mood is also important. Subjects find it easier to remember happy memories when they are happy and sad ones when they are sad (Anderson, 1995). Anderson's and Baddeley's findings may also suggest that revision for examinations is best done in the examination room and in the state the candidate is likely to be in on the day. Thus, it is unwise to drink and revise unless the intention is to be drunk when sitting the examination! So far, none of my students has turned up to the exam room drunk, they usually save this until afterwards. I can only presume that revision is also carried out in a sober state.

Because of the limitations of working memory (WM) it is necessary to present items to the user in such a way as to minimize failure. For example, for most people, passwords need to be kept to not more than nine characters (the magic number 7 plus or minus 2). The need to remember information for later input must be kept to a minimum so as not to overload WM. This means that the computer system should not ask for any information that is unnecessary nor should it request any information that it can derive. After each complete operation there should be some operation that will act as closure and offer feedback to the user. It is important that the user's memory is not overtaxed.

Furthermore, it is important to ask for material that is relevant. Users are much more likely to co-operate with a computer system which makes requests they can see the point of. Being asked for irrelevant information causes irritation and is not likely to help the user to learn how to operate the system. It is very easy to be irritated by forms which ask questions which the person filling it in might consider irrelevant or perhaps even impertinent! Computer systems should avoid placing unnecessary burdens upon the user and should avoid causing irritation or annoyance.

> One of my friends, married for over 40 years, now refuses to provide her maiden name. She has no idea what relevance a name she held for eighteen years, all that time ago, can possible have. She quite rightly concludes that it can be of no possible use or interest to anyone but herself.

It is possible to train the memory to perform remarkable feats. However, generally speaking, in the design of computer systems it is desirable to reduce any such need. The users should not be asked to do things that would cause them to have to tax their memories unduly. Some people might find it easy to recall several chunks of information while others would not be able to perform the task at all.

in yellow and so on. Then make a list of multi-coloured nonsense words. Try reading out the words on each list and then try saying the colours they are written in. You will probably experience some difficulty. This phenomenon is called the *Stroop effect*. The Stroop effect recognizes that once people have learned to read, they have a tendency to read whatever is put in front of them and when faced with two contradictory sources of information, in this case a colour written in the wrong colour, there is a conflict. Try this out on other people.

It is important not to think of interaction between the computer system and the user in isolation. The user is not just a user of the computer system but an employee with a telephone extension, a national health number, a tax code, a home address and telephone number, a bank account, a list of birthdays to remember and so on. Don Norman in his marvellous book 'The Design of Everyday Things' has a good deal to say about the number of things that the average person is expected to remember (Norman, 1990). The student of HCI would be wise to take his comments on board. In what he has to say about the difficulties of remembering all those numbers and information he speaks for a lot of us!

> I have a good memory for poetry but when it comes to remembering my own phone number I experience great difficulties. When I have recently moved house I can use that as an excuse but the rest of the time, there is no easy explanation. I can hardly move house every 6 months to provide myself with a suitable excuse! I have found it embarrassing in the past because people expect me to know. Nowadays, I carry the number around in my diary and I do not bother with embarrassment or excuses. What is the point. Don Norman has released me from all cares on that score and when it comes to things I find it hard to remember, I write them down and can say along with Henry Jones the elder in *Indiana Jones: The Last Crusade*: 'I wrote them in my diary so I won't have to remember them.'

3.7 Computer–human systems?

This is not a complete list of all of the aspects of human beings that need to be considered in the design of human–computer systems. It does not take into consideration all human capabilities and if a picture of a human being was drawn from an examination of present computer systems it would be assumed that the eyes were the most important aspect of the user. Such a drawing would also show that the fingers were all the same length, hearing was very low tech and there were no other senses or limbs.

Although this is the current state of play it does not mean that there might not be changes to the way in which future computer systems are built. For example, the feet could be used in future human–computer systems more than they are at present. Most people are able to use their feet when they drive a car and feet can be used to control quite sensitive controls. Kroemer has shown that people can be taught to use their feet to manage controls almost effectively as they can use their hands (cited by Oborne, 1995). Oborne remarks that hands, like the visual system, are almost always overloaded, so effective use of foot controls might be desirable (Oborne, 1995).

Special computer systems do exist for use by those who are unable to use conventional systems. Quite often these systems use human abilities which are not generally well developed in the majority of the population and these other methods of control can become quite highly developed in those people using them. For example, artists are able to paint with the mouth or the feet. Keyboards can be operated with a plunger held on the head but for the majority of people though, these skills do not exist.

However, an understanding of the present state of technology used in the construction of current systems should not prevent us from thinking about other ways in which interaction between computers and their users could take place. It remains necessary to see the human being as an entirety with other talents which are as yet unused or underused by modern computer systems. The student of HCI should be prepared to think of other means of interaction and should also be prepared to move with the times.

3.8 Summary

WM is limited and information decays rapidly unless rehearsed. Remember the magic number 7 plus or minus 2. More can be remembered if it can be chunked.

Human memory is more effective if it is given an appropriate cue.

LTM is probably infinite but associative and time is needed to retrieve items from LTM to WM. This slows down the time taken to perform a task. Items already in WM can be processed more quickly.

Closure is important especially where novice users are concerned since it tells them they are on the right track and releases them from the burden of having to remember the last piece of information.

Cues should come from the machine, especially for novices since often they do not know what they need to do next. Asking novices to remember such things increases the burden on memory.

Do not ask the user for any information that can be derived, or information that is out of sequence with the user's expectations. All of this will overtax the user's memory and will eventually cause irritation and annoyance.

Finally, it is as well to remember that memory is an extraordinary phenomenon and generalization is quite difficult. People can seem to have good memories for one thing and be quite bad at remembering something else.

3.9 Self test list

activation
chunking
closure
digit span
episodic memory
free recall
long term memory
magic number
primacy effect
recency effect
semantic memory
sensory memory
short term memory
Stroop effect
working memory

3.10 Exercises

1 Examine your favourite and not so favourite applications. What sort of demands do they make upon you as a user? Are you expected to remember more than is reasonable?

2 Make a list of things that you forget in a week. Is there any sort of pattern? When and why do you tend to forget things?

3 Make a list of common short cut keys and the tasks they represent. Give either list to your chosen subjects and see if they can provide the rest of the information for example if given a short cut key they can provide the task or vice versa. Try jumbling both lists and see if subjects can match them. You might like to compare these performances with asking users to show you the short cut keys on the keyboard.

4 Figure 3.6 shows the interface for a game called Memory Test. The user clicks on a tile to make the tile flip and reveal a picture. The user can display two pictures at any one time. Figure 3.7 shows the game with two tiles flipped and some tiles removed because they have been properly matched. The pictures are shown for 3 seconds before the tile flips back to the state shown above in the illustration. The object of the game is to match identical pictures. The user has to remember the location of each picture then click on the pair of identical pictures. In the example above there are 60 tiles, thus 30 different pictures. These pictures are fixed in that each separate game uses the same 30 pictures but their positions will change from game to game. The user is given a

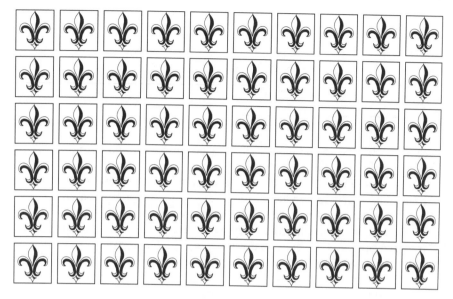

Figure 3.6 *The interface for Memory Test*

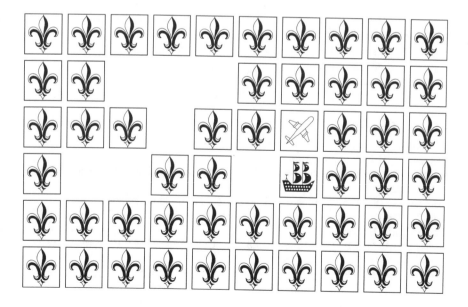

Figure 3.7 *Memory Test with some tiles matched*

Subject number	Trial 1	Trial 2	Trial 3	Trial 4	Trial 5
1	55%	58%	57%	45%	37%
2	45%	43%	48%	40%	30%
3	55%	45%	43%	34%	35%
4	27%	40%	40%	39%	35%
5	32%	33%	35%	33%	32%

score at the end of the game. There is no time limit apart from the limit to the time each tile is displayed.

The table above shows the performance of five subjects over five trials. The trials are conducted under the same laboratory conditions. The subjects are all volunteers. None of them have ever used or seen Memory Test before the trials. The percentages show the score for each trial and are based on how many times the subject examines a particular tile.

(a) Comment on the performance of the five users. Explain, with reasons, what you think is happening.

(b) Three further trials are run with the same five users. However, this time random sounds are assigned to the tiles. What would you expect to happen to user performance and why? If sounds were not random but associated with particular pictures what would happen and why?

(c) The pictures on the tiles are changed. The same users perform five more trials. What would you expect to happen to user performance and why?

(d) The pictures stay in the same position over the next five trials. Explain what will happen to user performance and why.

3.11 References

Anderson, J. (1995) *Learning and Memory*, Chichester: Wiley.

Baddeley, A. (1990) *Human Memory: Theory and Practice*, Hove: Lawrence Erlbaum Associates.

Baddeley, A. (1994) *Your Memory: A User's Guide*, London, Penguin.

Freud, S. (1901) *The Psychopathology of Everyday Life*, translated by Tyson, A. (1971), New York: Norton.

Loftus, E. F. (1979) *Eyewitness Testimony*, Cambridge, MA: Harvard University Press.

Miller, G. (1956) 'The magical number seven plus or minus two: some limits on our capacity for processing information.' *Psychological Review*, **63**, 81–97.

Norman, D. (1990) *The Design of Everyday Things*, New York: Doubleday.

Oborne, David J. (1995) *Ergonomics at Work*, 3rd edn, Chichester: Wiley.

3.12 Further reading

Anderson, J. (1995) *Learning and Memory*, Chichester: Wiley.
This is full of good examples and offers a detailed and integrated approach to memory and learning.

Baddeley, A. (1994) *Your Memory: A User's Guide*, London: Penguin.
This is undoubtedly the best book to read on memory. It is highly entertaining and readable.

Baddeley, A. (1990) *Human Memory: Theory and Practice*, Hove: Lawrence Erlbaum Associates.
This is a more detailed approach to memory. Again, it is highly readable but it is designed as a psychology text book so is perhaps a little drier than *Your Memory: A User's Guide*.

Gleitman, H. (1992) *Basic Psychology*, 3rd edn, New York: Norton.
It has lots of examples and some interesting exercises and has good sections on memory and the brain.

Rose, S. (1992) *The Making of Memory*, London: Bantam.
This book is an account of the biological makeup of the brain and memory. It isn't for the squeamish!

CHAPTER 4
The interface

Chapter overview

This chapter looks at the purpose of interfaces and methods of classifying them. It examines the methods of communication between user and system and looks at the differences between direct manipulation and linguistic manipulation. It establishes criteria for the development of suitable interfaces.

4.1 Background

The human–computer interface mediates between the user and the computer system. It protects users from the harsh realities of the system, reflects the system model to them and translates their intentions into appropriate system activity (see Figure 4.1). The user forms a model, known as the user's mental model, of how the application works. This model forms the basis of future interactions with the system and enables users to predict system performance. A detailed examination of the psychology of the user's mental model is beyond the scope of this book. However, at this point, it would be useful to accept that users form impressions of how systems operate, or better still that systems were able to adapt to the users' models. A more detailed account of mental models can be found in Norman's *The Design of Everyday Things*.

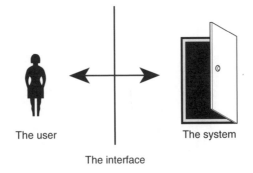

The user   The system

The interface

Figure 4.1 *The role of the interface*

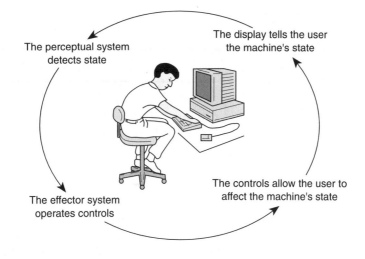

The perceptual system detects state

The display tells the user the machine's state

The effector system operates controls

The controls allow the user to affect the machine's state

Figure 4.2 *The human–machine loop*

Since mental models vary from user to user, change for individual users over a period of time, and may perhaps contain untenable expectations, the human–computer interface must help users to acquire an accurate model of the computer system. It must also accommodate different types of users, from novice to expert. This implies an understanding of both the user and of the task being performed. The classification of users will be considered in a later chapter.

Figure 4.2 shows a simple relationship between a computer system and the user. The user's perceptual system receives information from the machine via its displays. The user affects the state of the machine by manipulating the machine controls. The user and the system operate inside an environment and this can have an effect on the efficiency of the system. The impact of the environment will be examined in a later chapter.

The principles of interface design will be considered in the following sections. A list of guidelines will follow.

4.2 The principles of interface design

Naturalness

A good interface appears to be natural, it should seem to be an appropriate way of performing the task. The interface should reflect the user's task syntax and semantics: it should be in a natural language for the task involved and should appear to be structured according to that task. It should adopt an instructional tone since it has been shown that users become discontent with systems that try to be personal (Shneiderman, 1992). It should be self explanatory and idiomatic. It should not use the jargon of information technology (IT) but it might well use the jargon of the user's task since that is the language the user is familiar with. A good user interface should avoid any human pre-processing and human post-processing. In other words, the interface will not require the user to do something to the information before it is entered into the system nor do something to the information when it emerges. The system should adapt to the needs of the user and not expect the user to adapt to its needs.

Consistency

The interface should reinforce the user's expectations from any previous interaction with that system or indeed with similar systems. It should be consistent in its requirements for input and have consistent mechanisms for the user to make any demands on the system. The language of system messages and the system prompts should always be the same and should be in the same place where this is possible. The same methods should always be adopted for the selection and the termination of input from the user or for the cancelling of commands. The user should not be expected to learn one method for one area of the system and then another for somewhere else.

One of my students developed a new interface for an existing expert system. The original interface to that expert system was amazing in its number of modes and its methods of quitting from one part of the system to another. Sometimes you pressed control z and at other times control q or control x. Presumably, whoever had designed that system had designed each section in isolation. The overall effect was not considered and the result was a nightmare.

The output screen format should be consistent throughout the application. Any changes to the format should be done for good reasons and should be obvious. Small changes are unlikely to be detected by the user so if a change is needed then it should be very obvious.

There should be a consistent format for menus, messages and so on. There should be a consistent use of highlighting for attention when necessary. The user's attention should not be sought without good reason and when that attention is sought it should always be done in the same way. The interface should offer no surprises so the user should not have to guess why something has happened or what should be done next.

Relevance

The interface should not ask for redundant material. It should require the minimum of user input and should provide the minimum of system output necessary for the completion of the user's task. The user does not have time to read a lot of unnecessary material so on-screen information should be short and relevant but at the same time it must make sense. Making sense to the design team is not the same as making sense to everyone else.

There should be the minimum keyset/keystroke effort. This will maximize user performance and prevent unnecessary errors from occurring by reducing the number of potential key presses. This is especially important where the user is not a proficient typist. Novice users can make very slow progress if they need to hunt for keys. The system should not offer or request anything that it can derive from previous inputs, or anything that will not be used. Anyone who has filled in forms with irrelevant questions will know how important it is to keep requests for information to the minimum and to request only those pieces of information that are vital for the accomplishment of the task. Information requests should also be obvious and relevant: there is nothing more frustrating than filling in information the relevance of which is unclear.

The system's output should be simple and easy to understand. It is easy to develop a system that frightens users; the hard part is building a system that makes them comfortable and content.

> When we used Ada on the VAX to teach our first year students on the software development course they were always appearing in my office with plaintive requests for help when their program did not compile. Quite often, the compiler told them there was a problem and even explained what the problem was. However, the students did not usually read it. When I asked them what the error message was they did not know. The compiler was very helpful and told them their error in both jargon and plain English. Unfortunately, the student saw the jargon and was quite understandably frightened by it all.

A failure to provide a simple system shows that emphasis has been placed on making technical implementation easy rather than on the user's needs and comfort. Obviously, human–computer systems require the emphasis to be placed firmly on the user's needs; the whims of its developers must be subjugated to that requirement. Anyone who has learned to use a programming language to develop programs will know how unforgiving those first programs can be. This is because new programmers are not able, as yet, to consider the needs of the user because the actual building of the program is too intellectually challenging. However, proficient program developers do not have the luxury of being able to excuse themselves in this way.

Supportiveness

The interface should provide adequate information to allow the user to operate and to perform the task. This means that the system should provide sufficient specific help in order to help users formulate input requests. There should be adequate status feedback which should provide information to help the user continue with the task. For example, the sort of questions the user may well want answered are:

- Where am I?
- How did I get here?
- What is happening?
- Where can I go next?
- How do I get there?
- What can I do?

Where there is insufficient support for the user and the task being performed, the development team have failed to ascertain the requirements of the different users and their various tasks. Obviously, naive users need much more help than do experts. A good development team will know well in advance what the user is doing and the level of understanding the user has of both the task and the system. The subject of user types and their requirements will be discussed in the next chapter.

Flexibility

The interface should accommodate differences in user requirements and also in user preferences and level of performance. This will mean that the system needs to preserve consistency for the individual user, while at the same time recognizing that so far as different users are concerned there may well be a need to tolerate a wide range of input syntax and semantics.

The interface will also need to provide a variety of support levels and should also allow personalized output formats. In other words, the system should gear itself to the range of needs required by the different user types and their tasks.

At the same time, it has to be remembered that encouraging users to develop individualized interfaces means that they are less able to help each other. The advantages of personalized formats must be weighed against the disadvantage of being unable to support other users. If users do personalize systems there must be a way of recapturing the original information the interface operated with. For example, the VMS/VAX system allows users to create their own commands. If they forget these commands they need only to look at their configuration files to find out what the commands were. However, the normal VMS commands still apply. Microsoft Word allows users to define their own commands and short cut keys. These can be examined at a later date if the user forgets what they were, and as an aid to memory, can be added to the menus.

Some organizations actively discourage their employees from personalizing their systems as they do not want individualized systems to be developed. It can lead to a lot of problems if staff leave once they have set up parts of the system to their liking. Also, if systems are added to by helpful system administrators, it can lead to a complexity out of all proportions to the needs of the users. The London Ambulance Services Computer Aided Despatch system suffered from this very problem during its development (LAS, 1993).

> One employee told me that he had requested that a function be installed on the system. After this had been done for him, he promptly left. He remarked that the particular function would have no possible use for anyone else. That system will rapidly approach nightmare proportions if the system administrators continue their policy of helping the user to this extent.

4.3 The classification of interaction styles

There are two major means by which the user can communicate with a computerized system. Either the process could be carried out by linguistic manipulation, that is by typing in commands or it can be done by the direct manipulation of objects, that is by using some sort of pointing device.

The first type of interface is a command language interface and the second the graphic user interface (GUI), iconic interface or direct manipulation system. The vocabulary for the command language systems could range from a highly restricted code set through a limited subset of written language to a complete natural language interface.

The type of interface constructed will dictate the levels of support that will be available to the user and will dictate the nature of the input required from the user. It may also dictate the method of input be it via keyboard, mouse, touchscreen and so on.

There are several ways in which communication can take place between the user and the system. A command language interface could consist of a simple prompt which expects the user to input an appropriate command. This can range from a restricted set of inputs which may have to be input in a special way to complete natural language input. It is more likely to lie between these extremes. These interfaces are frequently referred to as command line systems because the current state of play is shown one line at a time.

Communication could be carried out on the basis of a conversational question and answer structure, again with the full range of vocabulary available to the user. Some query systems, such as a library cataloging system, operate like this. The system could be menu driven either on-line or otherwise. The automatic teller machines used by the banks operate like this. Finally, communication could take place via form filling interfaces or dialogue boxes. These are found on the World Wide Web (WWW), for example.

Any of these structures could be driven by mouse or by keyboard though some structures lend themselves more easily to one or the other. Table 4.1 summarizes these communication types.

Table 4.1 *Communication types*

Interface	Prompt	Language Set	Input Device	Examples
Command line	Cursor	From restricted to natural language	Keyboard	UNIX, MS DOS
Question and answer	Cursor with text prompt	Natural language	Keyboard, mouse, touchscreen	Booking system
Menu driven	Cursor, pointer, text prompt	From restricted to natural language	Keyboard, mouse, touchscreen	ATM
Form filling	Cursor, text prompt	From restricted to natural language	Keyboard, mouse,	WWW

The choice of the dialogue structure will determine the basic support level provided by an interface. This is an important consideration in the design of systems since it will affect the design of the interface. The level of support to be provided might be dictated by the type of user the system is aimed at or the sort of task being performed.

The conversational techniques considered in this section are:

- question and answer
- menu
- form
- command language systems

Most dialogues are a mixture of all these various techniques thus reflecting the varying nature of the input data and the varying nature of user expertise. It would be wrong to assume that any particular method was always the best user interface. It depends on the user and it depends on the task. In other words it boils down to: Know the user. Know the task.

Interestingly enough, modern GUI interfaces quite often use some of the techniques of the command language system, for example the wild card indicated by the asterisk. This enables the user to choose a particular file type and is much faster than trying to select various files using a pointing device. An example is shown in Figure 4.3. The wild card enables the user to specify a particular file type. For example ***.txt** would select any file with the **txt** extension. In the example shown in Figure 4.3 the *.* would match all the listed files, whereas of the files shown **.exe** would match only **calcyear.exe**.

Question and answer

The system decides the nature of the next input by providing the question. It displays the prompt identifying the nature of the required response and the user has to input this information. The method of display can vary between teletype, page mode and pop up. Figure 4.4 shows an example taken from a game for the Macintosh. Here, the potential answers can be selected by clicking on the appropriate radio button. Figure 4.5 shows an example taken from a command

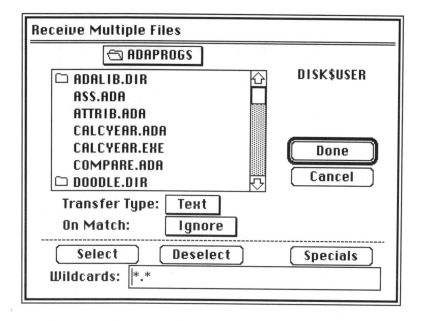

Figure 4.3 *An example of mixed input (Fetch)*

line system (MS DOS). The system has failed to read from drive a and needs the user to decide what to do next.

The input provided by the user is a single value and this value may be free format or from a limited set of possible inputs.

These dialogue types are moderately supportive of the user in that such a structure indicates the nature of the required response but not the actual value to be input. They are quite flexible in that they are able to handle a variety of input data types and accommodate short cuts. Question and answer dialogues can provide such facilities as defaults and answer ahead which will obviously

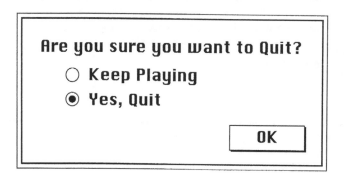

Figure 4.4 *Question and answer (GUI interface from Civilization)*

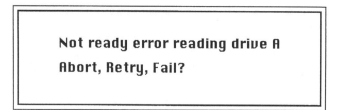

Figure 4.5 *Question and answer (command line interface, MS DOS)*

help the novice user (defaults) and provide accelerators for the expert user (answer ahead).

However, such a dialogue requires careful placing of prompts. It is also important to ensure consistency between the different areas of the interface in order to ensure success. Question and answer can be tedious and does sometimes lead to feelings that the system is in control rather than the user. It is important that the user understands the nature of the information that has to be supplied. It can be very frustrating for novice users who get stuck with a particular dialogue box because they are unsure what value the system is looking for. It is probably wise to provide defaults as a method of prompting the user for an appropriate value. However, question and answer dialogues can be quite useful for leading novices in the right direction.

Menus

Again, this is an interface type in which the system decides the nature of the next input. However, unlike question and answer, it displays a list of possible values in a variety of formats. Menus are so diverse today that it is not always obvious that what is being presented is actually a menu, the idea that a menu offered a choice of things to do has long since gone. Menus can offer a range of possible inputs, saving the novice user the task of trying to work out what sort of value might be required. The menu has the advantage that the user does not have to remember anything but merely to recognize it.

The types of menu available are many and varied. They range through all of the following examples:

- bar
- block
- button
- scroll bar
- full screen
- pop-up, pop-down, pull-down, drop-down
- tear-off
- walking menus (cascade menus)

Figures 4.6 to 4.8 show some examples of menu types.

Paint	Options

Select   ⌘S
Select All   ⌘A

Fill
Invert
Pickup
Darken
Lighten
Trace Edges
Rotate Left
Rotate Right
Flip Vertical
Flip Horizontal

Opaque
Transparent

Keep   ⌘K
Revert

Figure 4.6 *Pull down menu (from HyperCard)*

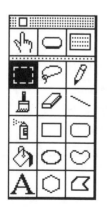

Figure 4.7 *Tear-off palette menu (from HyperCard)*

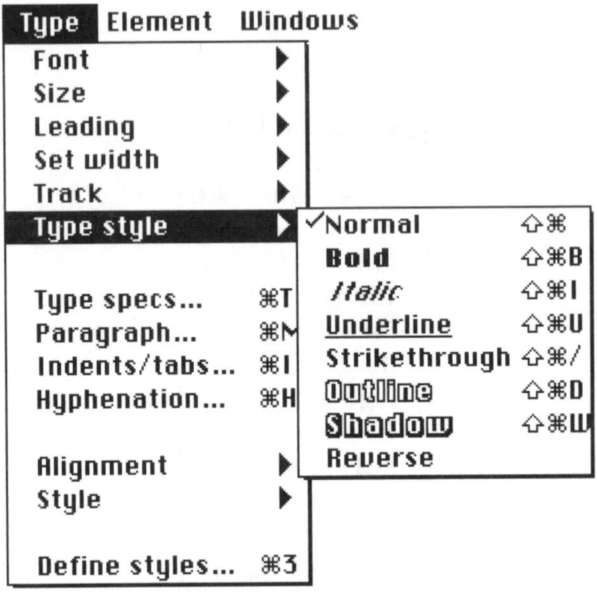

Figure 4.8 *Walking or cascade menu (PageMaker)*

The menu requests a selection from a list and the selection is made by:

- keying in an identifier
- scrolling down a list
- pointing to an item on a list

Figures 4.9 to 4.11 show some examples of the various input methods.

Menus can be found on GUI systems and command language systems. Selection is made in a manner appropriate to the particular system. A command

Figure 4.9 *Keying in an identifier*

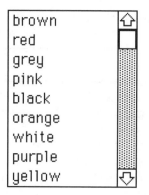

Figure 4.10 *Scrolling down a list*

language system may involve typing in an identifier, see Figure 4.9. A GUI is likely to involve pointing with a mouse or other pointing device, see Figure 4.10.

Menus are very supportive but they are do not provide flexibility. For example, only one selection can be made at a time.

There is a desirable number of entries for each menu which is determined by human cognition, for example. It is very useful to think in terms of the magic number 7 plus or minus two. If more menu items are needed than this

Family Members Listed

Click on name below to start

Dooly, Michael
Dooly Patrick Martin
Dooly, Terry
Faulkner, Maura Elizabeth
Faulkner, Neil (Snr)
Faulkner, Neil Martin
Faulkner, Nicholas
Faulkner, William
Hall, Alan
Hall, Charles (Jnr)
Hall, Charles Edward (Snr)
Hall, Christine Elizabeth
Hall, Joan
Hall, John Harry
Hall, Trevor John
Hall, Wayne
Jennings, David

Figure 4.11 *Clicking on an item*

then it is necessary to subdivide large menus and menu entries. Figure 4.6 shows a pull down menu with subdivisions. This means that large menus will have to be carefully ordered so that most frequently used items are at the top of a menu and each menu is grouped according to how the task will be viewed by the user. Large menus can create a problem in that it becomes difficult for the users to find their way around the system.

Some software developers have a way of naming menus which offers little in the way of guidance as to what might be found under that particular choice. Naming menu choices so that they are memorable, meaningful, obvious and brief is by no means an easy task. Different applications have tended to adopt different menu structures and sometimes these have been contradictory so that rather than positive transfer occurring the user has been faced with negative transfer. A menu choice (say paste) for a word processing package might not be in the same place or under the same main menu in a drawing package although standardization has gone a long way to curing these ills.

It is important that novice users are not faced with too many choices. It is easier to make a choice from a small selection rather than from a large one. It is only necessary to consider a restaurant menu to know how hard it can be to decide what to eat if the restaurant offers a very wide choice. For the novice user of a system, a complex menu can be equally bewildering. Some modern systems can use a technique of restricting the menu choices which are often called short menus and full menus. The system's functionality can be restricted in the early stages by selecting short menus. Once the novice user has grown accustomed to the system and needs the extra functionality then full menus can be selected. This can be a good technique to make a complex system seem more simple. It is rather like providing water wings for the novice swimmer or stabilizing wheels on a two wheeled bicycle for a new cyclist.

There has been some discussion over the relative advantages of broad or deep menu structures. Nielsen advises against hierarchical menus (Nielsen, 1993) but acknowledges in practice this is frequently impossible to avoid. The ordering of menus is equally controversial. Preece *et al.* (1994) suggest there are four real alternatives for ordering menu choices: alphabetical, categorical, conventional and frequency. Alphabetical requires no extra training, the user merely glances at the point in the list where the expected item is sought. In order to categorize menu items it is necessary to first define suitable categories and this can be controversial. The categories may not be obvious and some items might conceivably belong in one or more categories. Some menu designers overcome this problem by placing such items in more than one menu. But this can lead to confusion where the user is uncertain as to whether different options are on offer or it is merely the same option repeated. Ordering by convention means sticking to some pre-ordained order for example the days of the week. Ordering items by frequency of use first requires finding out how frequently different items are used and it is not always possible to predict this over a range of users with different tasks.

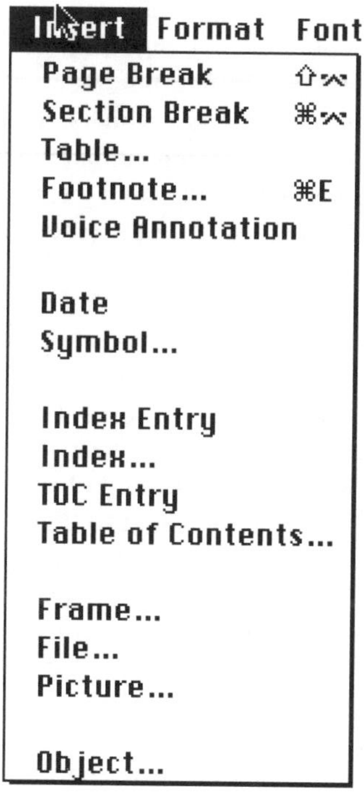

Insert	Format	Font
Page Break		⇧〰
Section Break		⌘〰
Table...		
Footnote...		⌘E
Voice Annotation		
Date		
Symbol...		
Index Entry		
Index...		
TOC Entry		
Table of Contents...		
Frame...		
File...		
Picture...		
Object...		

Figure 4.12 *The ellipsis indicating that a further choice has to be made (Word 5 on the Apple Macintosh)*

Where menus themselves lead to further dialogues this is indicated by the use of the **ellipsis**. Figure 4.12 shows an example.

Forms

The system decides the nature of a predetermined sequence of inputs and displays simultaneous requests for a complete set of inputs. Forms can consist of full screen or pop-up and each question may be answered by a question and answer, a switch or a menu. The user completes all input requests but the order in which this task is carried out is unimportant. The movement from one request to another is made by auto skip, where the cursor moves on when the field is complete, or manual skip, where movement is controlled by a control character or with a pointing device.

Users retain control of the form until they think it is complete and then offer it to the system by clicking on an acceptance button or pressing the return or enter key, for example. Most forms can also be cancelled, though this is not always the case. The system can provide validation of the various inputs by checking the values as they are input but more often, complete validation may not be attempted immediately but is deferred until the form is passed over to the system. At this point feedback may be given.

There are two types of forms: those which are designed for transcription input (that is, the screen matches a document that the user is working from) and forms which do not have corresponding documents. Where a form is used in conjunction with a printed document then the screen must match the document or errors are bound to occur.

These interface methods are very supportive but they are not very flexible. Short cuts can be accommodated by the use of defaults and abbreviations.

Care must be taken in the ordering and division of requests. The order must be logical to the users and must follow their idea of the task. Again, it is important to consider the positioning of those requests. Where input errors occur these need to be dealt with. The timing of error trapping is important. If the form is validated when the user sends it to the system then that could be a source of annoyance if an error has already occurred and the process of sending for validation causes unacceptable delays. Where possible it is better to trap each error as it occurs and to ensure that each input is correct before the form is sent to the system. On the other hand, errors can be trapped and corrected by default by the system. Obviously, the way in which this is dealt with will depend on what the user is doing, the level of user expertise and what is feasible. Incidentally, although automatically correcting user input to a default value that the system finds acceptable is one way of helping the user it can also be a source of frustration if the user does not know that the original value was not acceptable to the system nor why.

Forms have become much more important with the first generation of Web interfaces. Figure 4.13 shows an example of a World Wide Web form and Figure 4.14 shows an example of a typical set-up form.

Command language systems

Command language systems were one of the earliest forms of communicating with a computer. The command language system offers a prompt which can range from a dot to a word or short phrase. The system issues request for input via a prompt and the user decides the nature of next input. The input is a complete task request and consists of commands which operate upon objects of interest. In many ways the structure of the command language is like a sentence. It has a subject which is understood to be the system, it has a verb which is the action part of the command, for example **delete**, and an object which is the item of interest which is to be acted upon, for example **myfile.txt**. Figure 4.15 shows a screen from a command line system. The modifiers are like adverbs and adjectives. Input can be seen as commands for what is to be done and keywords to describe what it is to be done to. The command keywords or operations can be used with optional modifiers if necessary. What

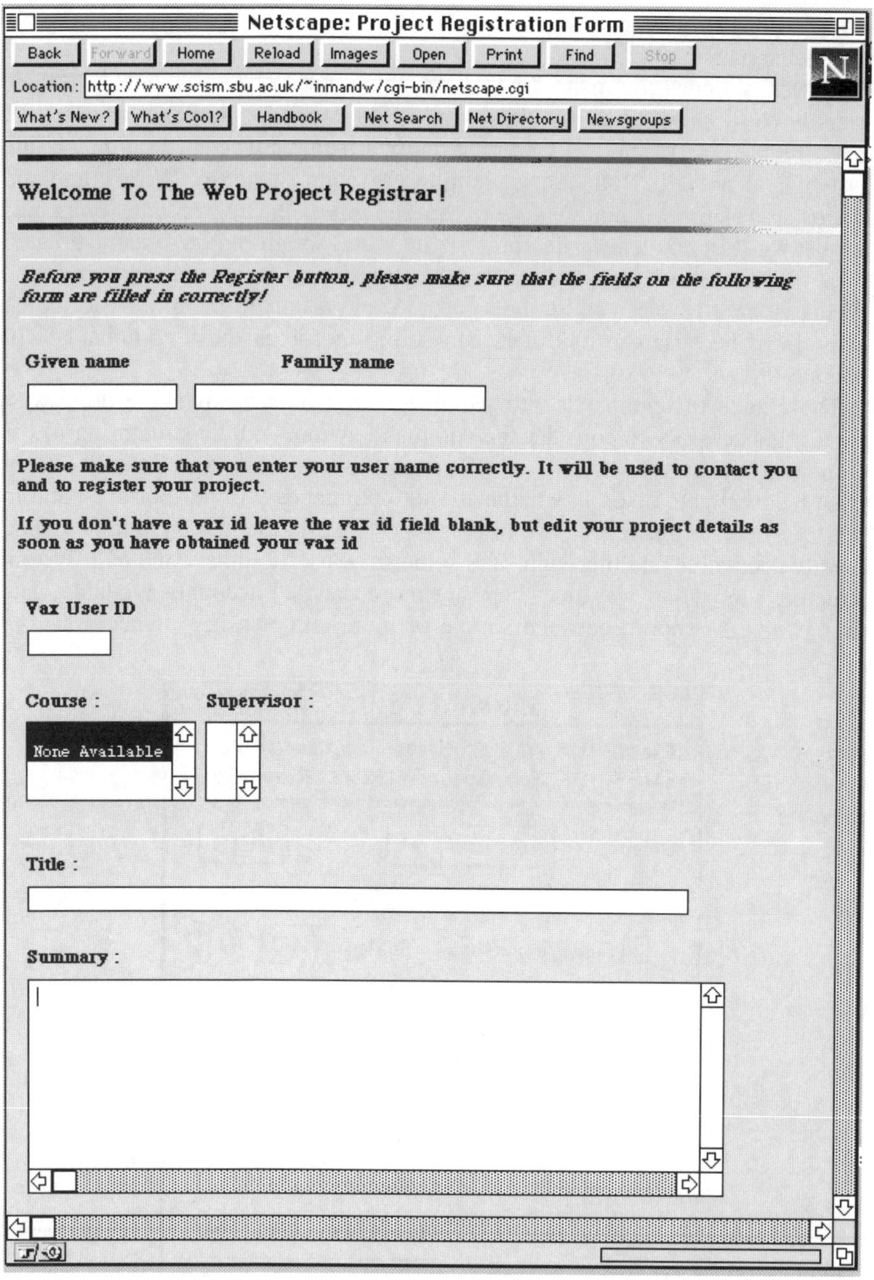

Figure 4.13 *A World Wide Web form*

is to be done to it is represented by positional parameter values and keyword/parameter pairs.

Generally, most command language systems are not very supportive since users have to know what it is they want to do and how they can achieve that goal. Figures 4.16 and 4.17 show a comparison between a command line system and a GUI. Both are presenting the same material. With command language systems it is not possible to proceed unless the appropriate commands are known. But conversely flexibility is high and should not be underestimated since the user is free to use commands, keywords and parameters so long as the syntax is what is expected by the system. Some tasks are therefore very quick to perform because the modifiers can select the areas these commands will operate on.

The choice of commands and parameter keywords needs to be done with care; it is necessary to consider the command syntax and the structuring of the command hierarchy. The choice of language is important and difficult. There must be great care taken in whether or not commands will be shortened and in what way. Error messages have to be supportive and the help system has to be readily accessible and thorough. It is sometimes useful to have the help system structured in such a way that there are more detailed accounts available. The user is able to choose between simple or more complex help if necessary.

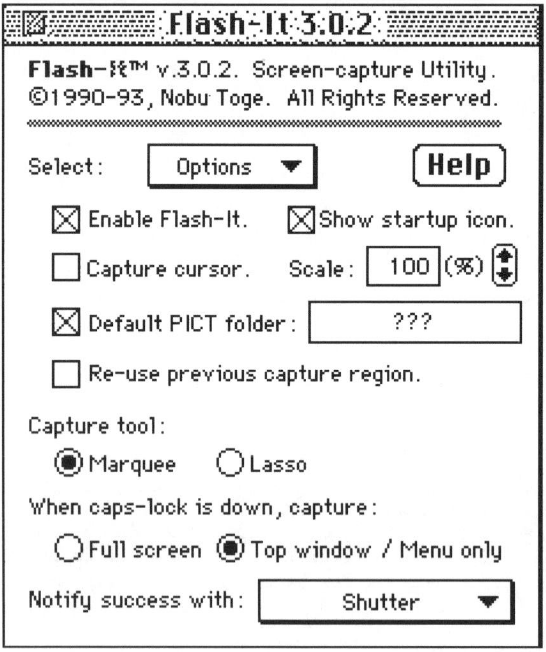

Figure 4.14 *A form for setting up Flash It on the Apple Macintosh*

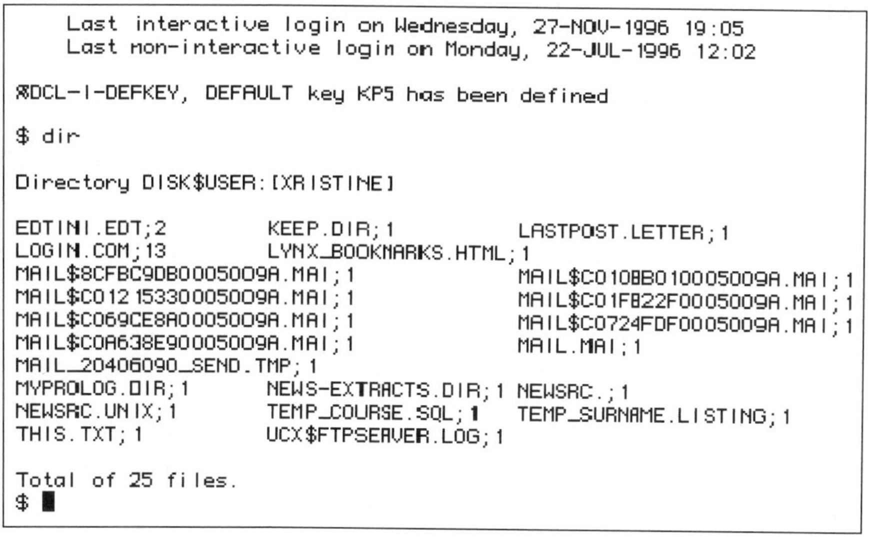

```
       Last interactive login on Wednesday, 27-NOV-1996 19:05
       Last non-interactive login on Monday, 22-JUL-1996 12:02

%DCL-I-DEFKEY, DEFAULT key KP5 has been defined

$ dir

Directory DISK$USER:[XRISTINE]

EDTINI.EDT;2           KEEP.DIR;1           LASTPOST.LETTER;1
LOGIN.COM;13           LYNX_BOOKMARKS.HTML;1
MAIL$8CFBC9DB0005009A.MAI;1            MAIL$C010BB010005009A.MAI;1
MAIL$C012 15330005009A.MAI;1          MAIL$C01FB22F0005009A.MAI;1
MAIL$C069CE8A0005009A.MAI;1           MAIL$C0724FDF0005009A.MAI;1
MAIL$C0A638E90005009A.MAI;1           MAIL.MAI;1
MAIL_20406090_SEND.TMP;1
MYPROLOG.DIR;1         NEWS-EXTRACTS.DIR;1 NEWSRC.;1
NEWSRC.UNIX;1          TEMP_COURSE.SQL;1   TEMP_SURNAME.LISTING;1
THIS.TXT;1            UCX$FTPSERVER.LOG;1

Total of 25 files.
$ ▮
```

Figure 4.15 *Example of a command line system (VMS/VAX)*

This is probably the most difficult type of interface to do well as there are many areas where grave errors can be made. A good command language system can be a joy to use because of the feelings of control it can offer the user, but sadly many command language systems are idiosyncratic to the extreme.

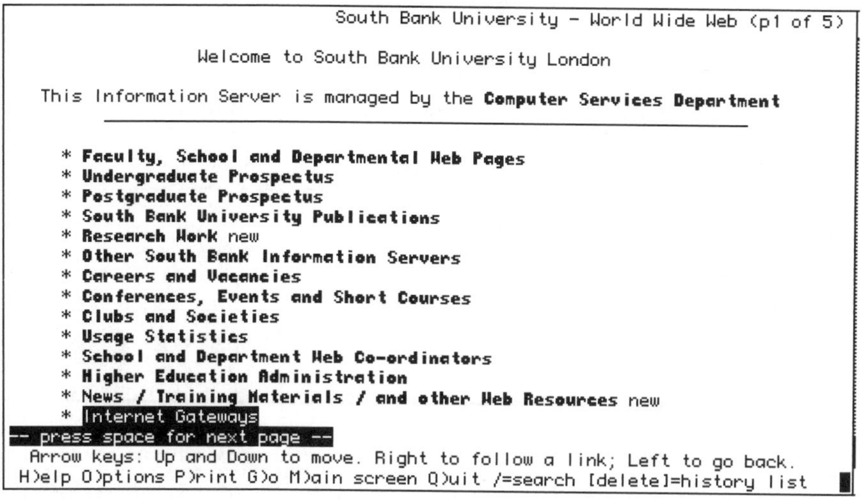

```
                    South Bank University - World Wide Web (p1 of 5)
               Welcome to South Bank University London

  This Information Server is managed by the Computer Services Department
  _____

        * Faculty, School and Departmental Web Pages
        * Undergraduate Prospectus
        * Postgraduate Prospectus
        * South Bank University Publications
        * Research Work new
        * Other South Bank Information Servers
        * Careers and Vacancies
        * Conferences, Events and Short Courses
        * Clubs and Societies
        * Usage Statistics
        * School and Department Web Co-ordinators
        * Higher Education Administration
        * News / Training Materials / and other Web Resources new
        * Internet Gateways
-- press space for next page --
   Arrow keys: Up and Down to move. Right to follow a link; Left to go back.
 H)elp O)ptions P)rint G)o M)ain screen Q)uit /=search [delete]=history list  ▮
```

Figure 4.16 *The World Wide Web using Lynx on a VMS/VAX*

4.4 Direct versus linguistic manipulation

The previous section considered the major aspects of interface design. This section examines some of the advantages and disadvantages of direct manipulation systems (GUI) and linguistic manipulation systems (command language systems).

Linguistic manipulation

Linguistic manipulation systems consist of issuing commands and providing labels for objects which those commands will operate on. Undoubtedly, considerable expertise is needed to move from the high level task concept, what is know as the semantic knowledge, to the associated sequence of system procedures or the syntactic knowledge. In other words, the task has to be translated into appropriate system commands which need to be remembered and typed in for the system to act. This puts a considerable burden on the user

Figure 4.17 *The World Wide Web using Netscape in the Macintosh*

of the system since the commands have to be learned. They cannot be deduced from interacting with the system.

Direct manipulation

This type of interaction provides a continuous graphical representation of current objects of interest that are physically manipulated by some sort of pointing device. There are labelled buttons to be 'pressed', icons can be dragged and their names overwritten. Menus can be pulled down and items selected. All manipulation is transparent and objects are represented by icons. Such systems can be seen as extended metaphors of the real world that they represent. Figure 4.18 shows an example interface from a game called Seahaven Towers. This consists of a click and drag interface which mimics a deck of cards. Metaphors are useful because learning involves the acquisition of new information into working memory, the retrieval of associated schemas from long term memory and the consolidation of new and old information into new schema. The generation of new metaphors is certainly an important part of the learning process. Principles are more readily absorbed from graphi-

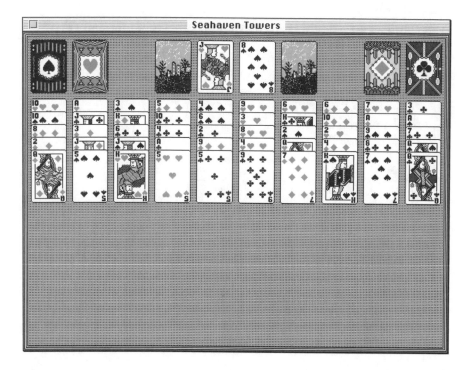

Figure 4.18 *Click and drag interface mimicking a deck of cards (Seahaven Towers on the Macintosh)*

cal representations of problems rather than from symbolic (linguistic) representations.

The iconic interface is designed to mimic familiar tasks and there are a variety of metaphors currently in use. The most obvious and common are:

- desktop
- paintbox
- spreadsheet

Figures 4.19 to 4.21 show examples of these metaphors.

Although graphical representations are easier to remember and recall than the equivalent linguistic token the icon still has to be interpreted accurately. In other words the user may well remember seeing an icon but that is no guarantee that its purpose will be recalled. Some icons are by no means obvious and even if the representation is recognized it does not mean that the functionality it supports will be obvious. For example, a piggy bank might be used as an icon to indicate a save function. The user might recognize the piggy bank but not guess that the functionality it supports is 'saving'. Figure 4.22 shows some

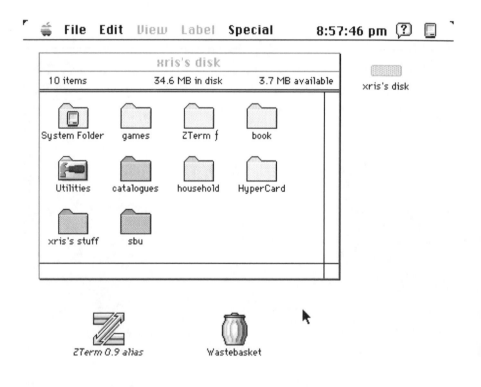

Figure 4.19 *The desktop*

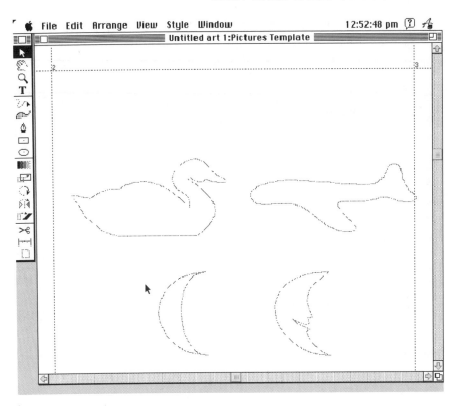

Figure 4.20 *An illustration package (Adobe Illustrator)*

examples of icons, some are possibly more obvious than others but it is likely that a novice user would be puzzled by many of them.

More importantly, there are no perfect matches available. For example, an icon must be selected before it is dragged. In the real world dragging and selection are much closer. There is no need to make the intention clear in two such separate steps. Furthermore, the user may well draw the wrong conclusions because of a misunderstanding of the metaphor or an interpretation of the metaphor that was not meant by the designer. For example, the user may use the wastebasket as temporary storage because a real wastepaper basket has been a useful temporary storage area in the past. The icons may not be understood by the user.

There is no guarantee that the iconic representation will be less verbose than the equivalent linguistic representations.

The advantages of the iconic interface are considerable. The user mimes the action by manipulating representations of objects. These actions have their equivalence in the real world. All this implies that the interface must support both continuous WYSIWYG (what you see is what you get) status feedback on

⌥	**File**	**Edit**	**View**	**Insert**	**Format**	**Tools**	**Data**	**Window**			12:49:38 pm	⑦	☒

Times New Roman ▼ | 12 ▼ | **B** *I* <u>U</u> | ≡ ≡ ≡ ⊞ | 🔗 % , | .00 .00 | ⊞ ▼ | ◇ ▼ | ☐ ▼

☐ 🖙 🖫 | 🖨 🖳 ✌ | ✂ 🖿 🖺 ⬭ | ↶ ↷ | Σ ƒ★ | 🔼 🔽 | 🔳 🔲 ⬭ | 100% ▼ | 💡 ▶?

| A1 ▼ | | BLUE SKY AIRLINES |

Blue Sky Sales

	A	B	C	D	E	F	G	H	I
1	BLUE SKY AIRLINES								
2	Sales Report								
3									
4		Region	January	February					
5		North	10111	13400					
6		South	22100	24050					
7		East	13270	15870					
8		West	10800	21500					
9									
10									
11									
12									
13									
14									
15									
16									
17									
18									
19									
20									
21									
22									
23									

◀ ◀ ▶ ▶|\ **Sales Report** / Sheet2 / Sheet3 / Sheet4 / Sheet5 / Sh|

Figure 4.21 *A spreadsheet (Excel 5)*

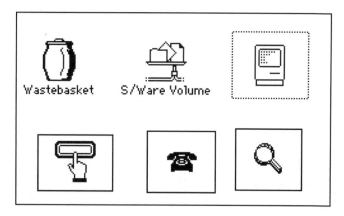

Figure 4.22 *Icons*

all current objects and reversibility of actions. Iconic interfaces are easy to learn since the operation of the system relies on task domain knowledge and this operation can be learnt by demonstration. It makes retention of knowledge easier for intermittent users since there is no syntactic knowledge to remember. The knowledge of the system is held by the system itself, it is knowledge in the

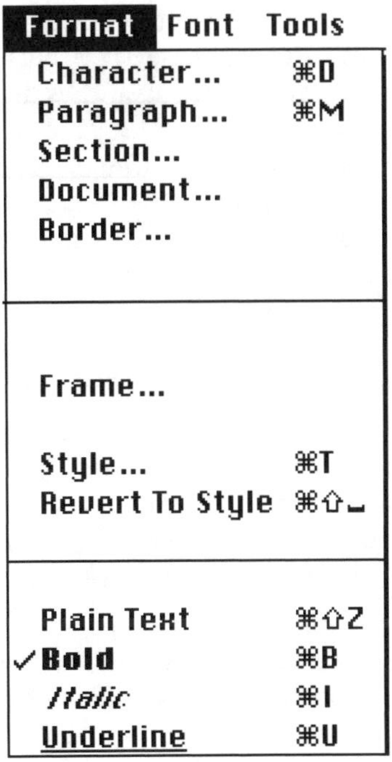

Format	Font	Tools

Character...	⌘D
Paragraph...	⌘M
Section...	
Document...	
Border...	
Frame...	
Style...	⌘T
Revert To Style	⌘⇧␣
Plain Text	⌘⇧Z
✓**Bold**	⌘B
Italic	⌘I
<u>Underline</u>	⌘U

Figure 4.23 *Example of menu and short cut keys (Word 5)*

world rather than in the user's head. Such an arrangement reduces the memory load on the user since whenever a task needs to be performed, an examination of the system will tell the user what needs to be done. The interface is consistent since it represents the current state and the user can confirm progress towards the goals and adjust behaviour if necessary. Status feedback is continuous and immediate. Because of this continuity of status representation and the WYSIWYG nature of the interface, there is easy reversibility.

Possible advantages of direct manipulation

These are debatable advantages with direct manipulation with devotees pushing them and direct manipulation haters pooh poohing them! It probably boils down to the nature of the task and preferences of the individual using the system. However, it is useful to be aware of the discussion.

Direct manipulation fans say that direct manipulation can be used rapidly by experts but it is true that for some things typing is quicker and shortcuts are not easily supported by a GUI. An examination of the short cut keys listed alongside the menus of a GUI wordprocessing package for example, will show that the short cut keys are many and varied. Figure 4.23 shows some examples. Furthermore, the shortcuts are not particularly logical and cannot therefore be derived from common sense. They have to be learned. Even worse, although there is now some attempt to make these short cuts consistent (e.g. on the Apple Macintosh, Apple control V might always mean paste) this has not always been the case. I know at least one Mac guru who has managed to learn a formidable number of short cuts but I would not suggest that most users cluttered up their minds with such nonsense!

It is argued that direct manipulation supports a wide variety of tasks but in reality it is seldom used for transaction processing and the limited set of operations represented by icons must be supplemented by quite large menus. Sometimes the structure of the menus can become quite large and GUI can still be forced into creating modes which are not transparent or obvious.

> For example, my favourite word processor package has menus which are now getting to the stage that they defeat me. This is particularly so because the particular software house keeps developing better and better versions and uses the opportunity to play leap frog with the menus. I wish someone would whisper 'positive transfer' into their ears.

Finally, some people say that direct manipulation effectively allows the elimination of error messages but the truth is that using direct manipulation they make different ones. However, it is possible to decide what sort of errors will be made and which ones will be eliminated. A user is still quite capable of deleting important and needed files in a GUI as in a command language system, or making the wrong menu selection, or opening the wrong package etc. Direct manipulation does not and cannot eliminate all user errors! It simply means that the user makes a different set of errors from the ones that would have made with a command language system.

> For example, my most common error using a GUI system is opening an important document whose structure I like, selecting all of it and deleting it then typing in a new document and saving it under the old document's name so that I overwrite the first, important document.

However, it is fair to say that the choice of the interface is an important consideration in deciding what sort of errors the user will make and that for some types of task the use of a GUI and direct manipulation might well reduce the occurrence of error.

Possible drawbacks of direct manipulation

It is argued that direct manipulation is based on a low-level of human intellectual development on the Piaget scale. Some people seem to think this is important. The same thing could be argued for a number of other activities. Personally, I do not need to be challenged by my computer interface, I have my video recorder to do that! However, I can understand that some people might feel that GUI interfaces talk down to them. If that might be a problem then another solution would have to be used.

Semantic errors are made rather than syntactic/lexical errors. It is a case of having to decide which errors the user will be permitted to make. It might be that the interface designer decides to prevent certain kinds of error from occurring.

Initial learning time is brief but it is necessary to consider the costs in terms of lost flexibility. The type of user is probably important here. If staff turnover is high then learnability might be the most important consideration. If speed is more important then an equivalent command language system might be faster.

There is the need to swap between keyboard use and the use of the pointing device. In the case of the mouse, some learning is required. Some people find it difficult to get on with. The skill does not come naturally!

I have noticed rather interesting working practices when keyboard and mouse have to be used at the same time. The keyboard often gets pushed close to the screen and the mouse moves to the front.

It could be that left handed users have an advantage here in that some of the left handed people I have witnessed using a keyboard have learned to manipulate the mouse in the right hand and can type with the left. I am uncertain whether they have simply given up trying to make mice obviously designed for use by the right handed work for them or they are simply more adaptable. Society is not particularly geared towards the left handed. Generally speaking, less than 10 per cent of any large national population is left handed (Oborne, 1995). Incidentally, some of my students carried out a small survey for me on left handed users recently and their findings confirmed my own informal observations.

It might be rightly conclude that direct manipulation is not superior to command language/menus but just different and it is necessary to consider the user's task before deciding which method would be best.

Not every user takes to GUIs and some tasks do not easily lend themselves to graphical representation. Some people find the icons difficult to remember and guess the meanings of.

Nowadays, it is unfashionable to be a fan of command language systems. But even so, it is important to see that the type of interface offered to the user has to be appropriate to the task that is being performed. The very best interfaces will be a mixture of the various techniques available, according to the task that needs to be done. They will not be a product of fashion but the result of careful consideration of both users and the tasks they are attempting to perform.

4.5 Some design considerations

The following sections look at some of the problems of designing for particular types of work.

Reaction time

Reaction time is between 150 and 200 ms (0.15–0.20 s) with 200 ms being typical. Reaction time can be affected by the following:

1 Simple auditory or tactile reaction time is approximately 40 ms faster than simple visual reaction time.
2 When a stimulus is not expected or occurs infrequently reaction time increases. A study by Warrick *et al.* (1965) showed an increase of 100 ms when typists were asked to press a button if a buzzer sounded without warning. The typists reacted more quickly if they were pre-warned.
3 Reaction time changes little between the ages of 15 and 60. More time is needed for those under 15 and there is a slight slowing of reactions after 60 (Keele, 1986).
4 Stimulus in the periphery of vision are reacted to about 15–30 ms more slowly than centrally presented stimuli (Keele, 1986).

Movement time

This is the time needed to make the physical response called for by the stimulus. It is a measurement taken from the beginning to the end of the movement.

Human beings can move in some directions more quickly than in others. For example, controlled arm movements based primarily on the pivoting of the elbow take less time than those requiring upper-arm and shoulder movement. These former movements are also more accurate.

Attention

Attention seems to be something that can be directed. For the purposes of designing computerized systems for people, the following forms of attention can be examined:

- selective attention
- focused attention
- divided attention
- sustained attention (monitoring or vigilance)

It is important to remember that where systems do not take into consideration the user's capabilities, stress is likely to be the result.

Selective attention

Selective attention requires monitoring several channels of information in order to perform the task. As the number of channels increases so the individual's performance decreases. When people have to sample several channels they tend to sample those in which signals occur frequently rather than those where signals occur infrequently. Furthermore, the limitations of human memory cause people to forget to sample channels when many are present. People also tend to sample sources more often than would be necessary if they remembered the status of that source when it was last sampled.

Under stressful conditions, fewer sources are sampled and those that are sampled tend to be the ones perceived as being the most important. The actual importance of the source might not be as perceived by the end user.

Guidelines for selective attention
- The number of channels to be scanned should be kept to a minimum.
- The relative importance of the various channels should be made clear.
- The environment should be as stress free as possible.
- Information should be available as to where the next likely source of information will be.
- Users should be trained to scan effectively.
- Multiple channels should be as close together as possible.

Focused attention

The problem in designing for focused attention is to maintain the single channel of information without distraction. The ability to focus attention depends on the proximity in space of the sources of information. It is difficult to focus attention on one source if others are within one degree of the visual angle from each other. The designer of a system requiring focused attention should endeavour to make the information as distinct as possible so that the user is not confused by the various channels nor do those channels compete for attention or become muddled in the user's mind.

Guidelines for focused attention
- Competing channels should be as distinct as possible.
- Competing channels should be as far apart as possible.
- Competing channels should be kept to a minimum.
- The channel of interest should be bigger, brighter, louder or more demanding of attention.

Divided attention

Humans have a limited capacity to process information and that can be exceeded if several tasks have to be performed simultaneously. However, people do tend to try to do many things at once even if they do not make a good job of dividing their attention between many tasks. The more expert the behaviour, the more the likelihood of the user attempting to perform several tasks at once. When error occurs it might not be noticed and if it is it can lead to stress.

Guidelines for divided attention
- Potential sources of information should be limited as far as possible.
- The user should be encouraged to prioritize and prioritizing should be supported.
- The tasks should be as easy as possible.
- The tasks should be dissimilar in terms of input/output/modality so as to reduce the likelihood of confusion between them.

Sustained attention

The incidence of systems that require sustained attention or vigilance may increase as automated control systems increase.

Vigilance has been studied closely. Laboratory studies show a decline in speed of detection/accuracy as the task time increases. This occurs over the first 20 to 35 minutes of vigilance (Reason, 1990).

In real-life situations people perform better at vigilance. This could be accounted for by differences between laboratory and real-life situations. Perhaps the person performing a real-life task that requires sustained attention is able to summon up extra powers of care that the laboratory subject is not able to call upon. Or perhaps there are subtle and unnoticed differences between the laboratory task and the real-life situation. It is unclear why there should be these differences. There is not general agreement on why performance should decline during vigilance (Reason, 1990).

Vigilance can be extremely stressful.

Guideline for sustained attention
- Work–rest schedules should be provided and different tasks done in order to reduce the amount of time spent on vigilance.
- The signal should be as conspicuous as possible.
- Uncertainty about when the signal is likely to occur should be reduced.
- Artificial signals and feedback should be provided.
- There should be adequate training and the skills acquired should be maintained.
- Motivation is important.
- Environmental distractions and stress should be minimized.

4.6 Summary

The interface provides a means of interpreting intention and action between the system and the user. The more natural it appears, the less obvious it will be. Ideally, the user should not notice that it exists.

The interface should be easy to learn, transparent and obvious. It should not require the user to make undue effort to learn its operation. Ideally, there should be consistency between various parts of the interface and various interfaces to various applications.

There are several methods of representing functionality for the user. The various methods are not always interchangeable. It depends on the task being performed and the user.

Direct manipulation systems may be easier to learn but they are not without their problems. Command language systems can lack transparency but can be very efficient and powerful once they have been learned.

4.7 Self test list

ellipsis
WYSIWYG

4.8 Exercises

1   Examine the menus of an application that you know well. Look at the highest level of menus and attempt to list what you expect to find under each group.
2   Make a list of top menu items from an application and jumble up the lower levels. See if you can properly assign them. Try this exercise on someone else.
3   Imagine you are to help decide on the menu items for an electronic personal organizer. How would you structure the highest levels? What would each of the high level menus contain and why?
4   Draw up a suitable dialogue to capture information about printing. If you had to implement this as a menu how would you structure it?

4.9 References

Keele, S. (1986) Motor control in K. Boff, L. Kaufman and J. Thomas (eds) *Handbook of Perception and Human Performance* vol 2: *Cognitive Processes and Performance*, New York: Wiley.

Oborne, David J. (1995) *Ergonomics at Work*, 3rd edn, Chichester: Wiley.

Nielsen, J. (1993) *Usability Engineering*, London: Academic Press.

Reason, J. (1990) *Human Error*, Cambridge: Cambridge University Press.

Shneiderman, B. (1992) *Designing the User Interface*, Reading, MA: Addison Wesley.

Warrick, M., Kibler, A. and Topmiller, D. (1965) Response time to unexpected stimulii. *Human factors*, **7**(1), 81–86.

4.10 **Further reading**

Barker, P. (1989) *Basic Principles of Human Computer Interface Design*, London:
    Hutchinson.
Has interesting examples and some sound principles. It is a good follow up text.

Eberts, R. E. (1994) *User Interface Design*, Englewood Cliffs, NJ: Prentice Hall.
This is an excellent and interesting book on interface design. It is easy to read and
    Eberts is a refreshingly honest writer who is unafraid to express his opinions. It is
    well worth looking at.

Preece, J. *et al.* (1994) *Human–Computer Interaction*, Reading, MA: Addison
    Wesley.
Has interviews with top HCI experts and good exercises. There are several chapters on
    design.

Reason, J. (1990) *Human Error*, Cambridge: Cambridge University Press.
This is a book that I return to frequently and enjoy reading. He has some excellent
    advice, and stories to make you gasp with disbelief or laugh hysterically.

Shneiderman, B. (1992) *Designing the User Interface*, Reading, MA: Addison
    Wesley.
This remains one of my favourites for sheer readability. It is also very thorough.

Sutcliffe, A. G. (1995) *Human Computer Interface Design*, 2nd edn, London:
    Macmillan.
This has interesting chapters on interface components, interaction styles, dialogue
    design and presentation techniques.

CHAPTER 5

Designing systems for people

Chapter overview

This chapter offers a classification method for different user types. It also provides appropriate guidelines for the development of systems for each user type. The design process is examined along with suggestions as to how to produce suitable designs.

5.1 Background

The design process is highly complex and difficult. However, there are frameworks in HCI which will enable the designer to go about the task of producing a suitable system in a more structured way. In order to design an effective interface it is necessary to know the answers to some obvious and basic questions:

1 Who is the user?
2 What is the task?
3 What is the environment in which the system will operate.

The development of the human–computer interface will consist of the close consideration of its various aspects. The role of the interface is to provide a cushioning buffer between the user and the system. It has already been noted that it provides the system's half of a conversation with the user. In effect this means that it acts as a means of allowing the user to work with the system. It identifies the system's functionality and should allow the user to decide which aspects of that functionality are required. Secondly, it should convey the current state of activity to the user and make any observations on that state. Thirdly, the interface should also be a means by which users are able to organize what it is that they intend to do and how they will go about their tasks.

This chapter will commence with an examination of ways of categorising users into appropriate user types. This will make the task of design easier since it will answer the question 'Who is the user?' Secondly, the task will need to be examined and understood. A process of task analysis that has already been tried and tested elsewhere will help discover what the user is doing. In a later chapter, the concept of socio-technical design will be examined. This will help provide a more environmental and rounded view of the user and the task being performed. It will also enable the context of the task to be considered.

5.2 User classification

Earlier chapters have mentioned the different levels of expertise encountered in the user populations, but so far these levels of skill have not been considered in any detail, nor have the advantages of user classification.

For the sake of convenience, it is possible to categorize the user into user types. For example, so far as levels of system acquisition are concerned the following three categories of user could be identified:

- novice
- knowledgeable intermittent
- expert/frequent users

However, users can be classified in any other way that is appropriate to the system being built. This will depend on the nature of the users the system is designed for – the user population. For example, the users might all be novices but with different backgrounds so that then they could be classified according to whether or not they had keyboard skills or had used a computer before, to play games, for example. Of course, in extreme cases the nature of the user population might not been known and it will therefore be assumed that it might consist of any level of ability. In these cases artificial boundaries can be drawn as would be done if the design was aimed at the general public.

There is nothing to stop the designer of a system from designing for a particular category of people and ignoring different categories of user if this is appropriate. For example, if the system was always used by blind users then it could be decided that there was no need to design for sighted users.

The advantage of classification is that generalizations can be made about the users of the systems and their needs. At present it is not usually possible to design for individuals, but it is possible to classify individuals according to the various characteristics they might have and then design for those broad groups. Classification of users works in just the same way as classifying people according to the size of clothes they will fit into or the size of shoes they wear. It is a generalization of type but it does enable the designer to design for broad areas of performance. Of course, it does not mean that the best system has been designed for every individual. It means that the best system has been built for the generalizations identified as the appropriate user group. Particular in-dividuals might have very particular needs and may well not get on with a specific system at all, in exactly the same way that those who are very small or very large do not easily fit into the categories of shoes and clothes that are available in the high street. However, classification does not exclude designing for particular needs. If a particular type of user needs to be accommodated in the system then that particular category of user is simply brought into the design process and their needs are then considered.

5.3 User types

This section looks at the categories of users mentioned above and considers them in more detail. These categories are suggestions only and the actual categorization of the user population for the design of any particular system will involve a careful study of that user group and its classification into the various user types.

The following generalizations can be made about the user types so far identified.

Novice users

For the novice user of a computer system, processing is slow and laborious because of the limitations of working memory. Knowledge is declarative rather than procedural and the grouping together (chunking) of ideas is almost if not entirely absent. My students when asked to write down the operations they carry out in order to log on to the VMS/VAX via the School of Computing's terminals invariably produce the list shown as expert steps in Table 5.1. The actual steps shown in Table 5.1 would be how the novice would view the same operation.

Systems to be used by novices require more feedback and more opportunities for closure so that the novice feels that progress towards the goal is being made (this was covered in an earlier chapter) and is not left for long periods of time

Table 5.1 *Logging on according to the expert's view and the actual steps*

Expert steps for logging on	Actual steps for logging on
Input username	Press any key to activate screen
Input password	Press return to display menu
	Input manu choice
	Press return
	Input username
	Press return
	Input password
	Press return
	Wait for welcome message

wondering if what has been done so far is right as this might well cause anxiety.

Guidelines for novice users

Novice users present the most significant challenges when designing systems for people. Expert users have a way of sorting themselves out but novice users can rarely do that.

Guidelines for the production of systems for novice users might include the following:

1 *All initiatives should come from the computer.* The novice user will not know what can be done. Novices may or may not have a good understanding of the task domain but even so, the system needs to provide as much help as possible. It should offer things to be done and expect answers to questions. T. H. White in 'The Sword in the Stone' in describing the first meeting between Merlin and the young Arthur remarks that Merlin did not speak in questions so that there was little opportunity for conversation. The designer of a system should consider the novice user to be like a shy visitor who needs prompting so it is necessary to speak in questions.

2 *Each required input should be brief.* Input should be brief because the shorter it is the more likely it is to be remembered and the less likelihood there is of an error occurring when the user keys in the response. The opportunities for error by novices should be minimized. Designers should not assume that computer users are proficient keyboard operators.

3 *Input procedures should be consistent with user expectation.* The user should not be faced with anything that seems inconsistent or unlikely. Remember that humans search for patterns and will generalize. The system designer wants to make sure that the patterns the novice discovers really exist and are the ones the designer intended. In the absence of guidance, human beings will look for explanations of behaviour. It is important that the novice user forms an understanding that matches the system. Righting the wrong idea can be difficult and frustrating. Where possible it is sound practice to offer a metaphor that will enable a novice to formulate suitable ideas about the system and apply knowledge from other sources.

4 *No special training should be necessary.* A computer system should use knowledge in the world rather than knowledge in the head (Norman, 1990). In other words, all of the information needed to operate the system should be provided by the system itself. The novice user should not have to remember too much which means providing all the information that a user needs on the screen.

Most people do not worry about whether or not they will be able to negotiate every door they might encounter. They know that if they see a door it will open in one of a limited number of ways. They use the appearance of the door to give them a clue about how it might be opened.

Computer systems should be like that. Looking at the system should make it clear what has to be done and there should be no fears in the user's mind that failure might occur. Designers of systems should, where possible, use metaphors that the user will be familiar with. Figure 5.1 shows some controls that may suggest appropriate behaviour to the user.

5 *All system messages should be clear and unequivocal.* The user should not be left puzzling over the meaning of a particular message.

One error message I sometimes get when using the computers in my office is shown in Figure 5.2 'Can't open printer'. I love this message. I do not want the printer opened at all. I want to print something.

If a system can offer a puzzling message then it can certainly offer a clear one. A clear message to a computer expert is not necessarily a clear message to a beginner; it is important that messages are aimed at the appropriate level.

All messages to the user should be clear and to the point. That does not mean that they have to go into great detail. If users do not need to know something then there is no point in having them troubled by it. It

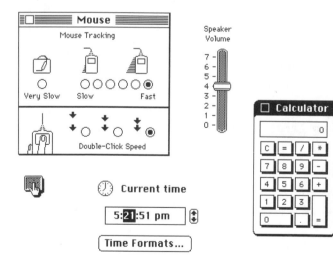

Figure 5.1 *Some controls*

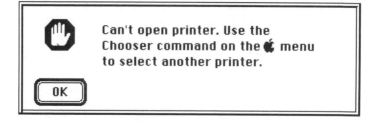

Figure 5.2 *Error message on a GUI*

will simply add an unnecessary burden to an already over-burdened memory load.

6 *User decisions should be made from a small set of options.* If you go to a cake shop and there are hundreds of cakes it becomes hard to choose the one you want. A small choice makes it much easier. Novice users need to make choices from a small number of options available since it makes them feel that the system is limited in size and it avoids feelings of being overwhelmed by the enormity of the system.

One method used in GUI systems is that of using a menu option for full and short menus, see Figure 5.3 for an example. Selecting the short menus option means that some of the options are hidden; this can

Edit Go		**Edit** Go Tools Paint	
Undo	⌘Z	Undo	⌘Z
Cut Picture	⌘X	Cut Picture	⌘X
Copy Picture	⌘C	Copy Picture	⌘C
Paste Picture	⌘U	Paste Picture	⌘U
Clear Picture		Clear Picture	
New Card	⌘N	New Card	⌘N
Delete Card		Delete Card	
		Cut Card	
		Copy Card	
		Text Style...	⌘T
		Background	⌘B
		Icon...	⌘I

Figure 5.3 *Short and full menus (Hypercard)*

be very useful for novice users. It hides functionality until the user knows a little bit more about the system. At the same time, the user can restore the availability of that extra functionality if need be and is left in control.

7   *Users should control the pace of interaction.* Novice users need to decide when they are ready to go on. They want to examine the screen as it is unfamiliar to them. They want to read all the words and look at everything. Telling a novice user that something is unimportant at the moment might well be true but the novice wants to see and wants to be in control.

An interesting experiment with babies showed that this desire to be in control of things was true at a very early age. Two sets of 2-month-old babies were given identical mobiles. One set of babies were able to control the movement of the mobile by turning on a switch underneath the pillow. If the babies turned on the pillow then the mobile was switched on for a second or so. The babies soon learned to move their heads from side to side on the pillow in order to switch the mobiles on. They seemed to be happy with the mobiles. They smiled at the mobiles and made noises that showed they were pleased. Another set of babies could not control their mobiles. The mobiles were operated automatically. After a few days, this second set of babies was no longer interested in the mobile. They did not smile and make noises at the mobiles when they moved. Although the mobiles turned about the same number of times for each set of babies, the babies in control of the mobile's movement stayed interested in the mobile longer. They appeared to enjoy controlling the movement (Watson, 1967; cited by Gleitman, 1992).

Control is probably, therefore, a deeply seated desire in human beings. We like to feel that we are in charge of a situation. Good computer systems give the feeling of control to the user. Designers should not guess how long a user needs to perform the task; the user should decide. For example, in direct manipulation systems the speed at which the pointer travels on the screen can be set by the user. The novice user of a mouse will probably be much more comfortable with the pointer travelling as slowly as possible. But as they become more expert they will very likely increase its speed to its fastest.

8   *User decision making should be in response to a specific request for action.* The user should not be expected to guess that it is now time to do something. Decision making needs to be prompted and the system should take the necessary initiative.

For example, tasks like saving a document may need to be prompted. New users are quite capable of quitting an application without saving the work they have just completed. The designer of a system should anticipate what will need to be done and get the system to prompt if something will need to occur, it should not be left to chance. If an error or omission is a possibility then someone sooner or later will undoubtedly do it. The task of the designer of a human–computer system is to avoid potentially 'dangerous' situations for the user.

9   *Help (human/machine/manual) should be always available.* It will probably come as no surprise that people prefer getting help from people. Novice users should not be left unaided, which does not mean that they should not experiment and explore. Assistants should not hover too obviously or too closely but they should be easily at hand.

When I taught a friend to use a word processor it was an uphill struggle. He hated the word processor and preferred a typewriter. I used to wait anxiously for the "beep" to occur knowing that it signified a problem. If two beeps occurred then I would get ready to appear as if by magic. On the third beep, I was there. It was a time consuming process but he is now much more comfortable about computer systems and I learned a lot about the way in which novices think about systems that are unfamiliar to them. Even today, after using the system for over two years, there are occasions when he needs help. The manual is quite good but that does not stop him from seeking human help. People understand problems better than manuals do.

10   *There should be sufficient feedback.* Novice users like to know if they are on the right track. There should be opportunities for closure to occur so that the novice feels comfortable about how things have progressed so far. In GUI systems the feedback can be graphical. For example Figure 5.4 shows the wastebasket before and after deletion has taken place. The user can see that the file has gone because the wastebasket goes from bulging to normal. Figure 5.5 shows the confirmation message issued when the user chooses the 'empty wastebasket' option. There is no reason that a command line system

Wastebasket

Wastebasket

Figure 5.4 *Feedback from a GUI system*

Figure 5.5 *The GUI confirmation buttons*

```
$ dir

Directory DISC$USER:[XRISTINE.LETTERS]

FTP.TXT;2        HCI.DIS;1        WEB.TXT;1

Total of 3 files.
$ delete *.txt;*
$ dir

Directory DISK$USER:[XRISTINE.LETTERS]

HCI.DIS;1

Total of 1 file.
```

Figure 5.6 *Feedback from a Command Line system. In this case the user, not the system, has initiated feedback*

should not confirm that deletion has taken place. On the VMS/VAX there is no such confirmation and users rapidly learn to use the **dir** (directory) command to list their files after copying or deletion. A sequence of commands for deleting files on a command line system is shown in Figure 5.6. For the expert the act of deleting will be chunked into the sequence shown in Figure 5.6. For the novice the sequence would consist of all those steps.

Knowledgeable intermittent users

Knowledgeable intermittent users are able to maintain semantic knowledge of both the task they want to perform and of the computer concepts involved. However, because their use of the system is intermittent they need consistent structures, good help facilities, and good documentation. Consistency is particularly important, as with infrequent use the idiosyncrasies of various parts of the system are likely to be forgotten and parts of the system might well be intermingled and merged in memory. If the system is consistent assumptions that are made about the various parts will hold true for the entirety so this merging of knowledge, if it occurs, is unimportant.

Documentation and help systems are particularly important to the intermittent user as they will know what they want to do and possibly the sort of process involved in carrying out the particular task but may need prompting on the details of how this will be done. Context sensitive help here can reduce the amount of time spent searching for the relevant help. These requirements do not contradict any requirements made for the novice user of a computer system nor indeed for an expert user either.

Expert users

Expert users will be well versed in both the semantic and syntactic aspects of the computer system. Their response time will be rapid and they will require brief feedback because they are accustomed to the performance of the system.

Experts organize their knowledge according to a higher conceptual structure. They are able to recall larger amounts of information than novices can because their knowledge is chunked. As a result of this chunking of information, low level, routine interaction sequences are compiled into high level procedures. Table 5.1 shows how that might operate. It is likely that experts will tend to have very similar mental models of the system, whereas novice's mental models will vary because they are based on past experiences of a diverse nature and not on past experience with the particular system. Indeed, the structural relationships of experts' cognitive representations of systems are fundamentally different from those of the novice.

Expert users of computer systems will typically look for abbreviated command sequences and will also want accelerators to take them through the dialogue sequences as rapidly as possible; for example, keyboard short cuts.

In fact, the requirements of an expert user are almost in contradiction of the requirements of a novice user. Luckily for designers of human computer systems, some of the design decisions made for the novice user will be chunked by the expert into part of a higher activity. For example, it is common to produce a confirmation prompt for 'dangerous' activities. In a GUI this may well involve clicking on the 'ok' or 'cancel' button or by pressing the return or enter key. In a command line system it will involve inputting a command and

```
$ delete/conf.*.*;*
DELETE DISK$USER:[XRISTINE]EDTINI.EDT;2?[N]:n
DELETE DISK$USER:[XRISTINE]KEEP.DIR;1?[N]:n
DELETE DISK$USER:[XRISTINE]LETTERS.DIR;1?[N]:
DELETE DISK$USER:[XRISTINE]LOGIN.COM;13?[N]:
DELETE DISK$USER:[XRISTINE]LYNX_BOOKMARKS.HTML;1?
```

Figure 5.7 *The command line confirmation (VMS/VAX)*

pressing return or pressing return to activate the default. Notice that in the command line system the user has to decide to activate the confirm option although in the case of the VMS VAX example (see Figure 5.7) delete could be redefined by the user as involving a confirmation request.

For the expert user, the activity of deleting a file will be chunked into a higher procedure that becomes the whole activity, including pressing the return or enter key. For the novice, this will not be the case. Of course, it is possible to overdo the 'Are you sure?' prompts and the system designers should consider very carefully what they hope to achieve with such a structure. In some situations it is more or less a complete waste of time and can be a source of much irritation. The problem is that they will be ignored and the expert will automatically confirm the dialogue box by pressing return. This means that the warnings may not register and the expert will end up doing something that was not intended.

Figure 5.8 shows an extract from one of the many e-mails I get on the subject of confirmation boxes. This expert is tired of confirming actions he knows he wants to make.

Some developers invariably develop systems with a lot of confirmation, even for the most trivial of requests. Try to seek confirmation only when it is important to do so. Sometimes the rare occurrence of an error is actually less irritating than the regular occurrence of a prompt to avoid that error.

5.4 The design process

In order to design a system, it is necessary first to understand what it is that the system should be doing. The process of understanding the job to be done by the system is provided by task analysis. This allows the major task to be broken down into its component parts. This process continues until the task appears to be a single building block. See Figure 5.9.

Task analysis

The design process will begin with an analysis of what needs to be done. For this the user's task will need to be examined in some detail.

Although it is more often the case now that the existing system will be a computerized one this is not always the case. The designer of a system might well be examining a manual system which is to be computerized. None of the recommendations here imply the examination of a computerized system or a manual system. The process will operate equally well upon either and will remain the same.

The following questions will have to be answered for each major task carried out:

- What does the performer of the task do?
- What information is used for each task?
- What affects task performance?
- What causes error in task performance?
- What are the good features of the present system?
    You will need to safeguard these if that is possible.
- What are the bad features?
    You will need to get rid of these.
- What skills are required for each task?
- How are these skills acquired?

Do you remember me saying some time ago that the most irritating feature of Eudora is its snivelling apology when there is no new mail "Sorry you have no new mail".

It struck me this morning that the message no longer bothers me. Why? Cos one simply checks the box and clears the screen with total disregard for the message. You don't read it! But you already know that happens.:-)

Why I have to check a box at all is a different issue. Same when there is mail. I have to check a box before I can get back into the programme to read the damn stuff. Humph!

It would be nice if the user options allowed one to amend text in the boxes or simply get rid of them.

Time for a campaign for simple screens. Just cos it's easy to make a button box is no reason to have one, they can get in the way especially when the little **** pop up over your applic and hang everything till you kill them.

Figure 5.8 *Extract from an expert's e-mail*

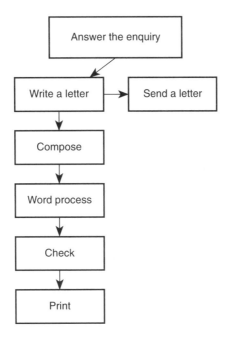

Figure 5.9 *Task analysis*

- How are these skills maintained?

As well as the task performed by the user there are transformations which alter the state of the task environment. These may involve other people or other machines. They need to be considered because of the way they can influence the way in which a task is carried out. Transformations can be influenced by

- environmental factors
- external procedures
- time constraints

Transformations have to be considered in designing a system since it is necessary to know what state the task and the object of the task is in at any given time. It is also important to know what causes the transformations to take place. Are they triggered by another human or another system?

Procedure for task analysis
Each task is a hierarchy of task and subtask. In other words tasks can be broken down to their simplest level of task.
    For each task define:

5.6 The purpose of task analysis

The process of task analysis should produce a clear understanding of what it is that the system must do. The next stage is to convert that understanding of the task into an appropriate human computer system. Here the concern is not with the development of a piece of software *per se*, but of its interface. There is insufficient time in a book such as this to consider the problems of software engineering in detail though undoubtedly the designer of the interface is likely to come across these problems and hopefully at an early stage in the development of the system. Furthermore, the HCI practitioner may or may not be a programmer. Software engineering is a much more careful and rigorous activity than it has been in the past, but a discussion of the methods involved is inappropriate at this point.

It is easier to identify what it is that makes a bad interface rather than explaining how to go about the task of building a good interface in the first place. In any case, sometimes it might be necessary to go against HCI rules in order to create a usable system.

> For example, one of my students created a drawing package for students with learning and motor difficulties. When he tested the system he found that the users accidentally quit from the application because he had kept all of the menu choices close together to reduce user effort. In the second prototype the option to quit was moved outside the main application window so that the users had to make a conscious and deliberate effort to quit. He would not have worked this out for himself without the experience of evaluating the system with the real end users.

Much of my time with students is spent in evaluating existing systems. This can sometimes be rather depressing for the particular student who has designed a system in that we tend to concentrate on what has gone wrong rather than what has gone right. The sensitive would have a short life span in HCI. But it also explains why the first version of a particular application is not the last. Bugs do get fixed, that is true, but these upgrades invariably add more functionality or play about with the way in which information is displayed on the screen. This happens because ordinary users make remarks, suggestions, complaints and so on and the developers are able to take these on board or ignore them as they see fit. The second system purchased is always better and more suited to the user than the first because the user has learned what parts of the first system were awkward to use or inappropriate.

> To my knowledge, my university has had four library enquiry systems. When I first used the system it was available on any terminal, all over the various sites. It was not all embracing but it was not bad. The next system was a nightmare from the user's point of view. It was available only in the library and so slow to use that you felt it must be tracing

every word with its finger. The latest system is much better. The library staff certainly learned through experience what was needed.

Sadly, in the case of HCI it is certainly much easier to criticize than to create in the first place.

However, it is not possible to simply evaluate and modify existing systems. Sooner or later a new system will be needed. Thus, if it is possible to identify the criteria that go together to make a good interface then perhaps, if this can be put together with a process, that will go part of the way along the road to find a good design method for the development of the interface.

The design of the interface will largely depend on what the task is and how the screen needs to look at any given time. If designers follow the rules of consistency then a screen layout designed for one aspect of the interface must have an impact on the screen design of another aspect. It is likely that the layout of the screen will be dictated by the kind of information displayed. The problems of lengthy lists of functionality have already been examined and ways suggested in which this can be controlled by the use of short or full menus, for example. The first problem then should be answered by the task analysis. What does the user want to do? The answer to this question should provide a list of functions. Once the designer of the system knows what the user wants to do then the design team can go about the task of designing an interface to support each of those tasks as appropriate.

The second problem is then that of how the task is going to be presented to the user. Some people refer to this as the aesthetics of the system. What they mean is how the task information can be presented to the user in a way that is pleasing and supportive. At this level it is necessary to consider those aspects of user physiology and psychology that were examined in the earlier chapters. For example, it might be wise to subdivide the tasks according to a structure that will aid the user in learning how to operate the system. The menus will consist of items that are linked and meaningful. Names that are appropriate to both task and user will be chosen. Some of this information will be prescribed by the particular user and the particular task. For example, if the task was to design a system to help a graphic designer then the team would need to know the sort of structures that the graphic designer would want to manipulate. The system would use the user's language and tools. Furthermore, it would be necessary to consider how much can be displayed on the screen – it is important to avoid screen clutter and details such as colour, font, line size, window size and shape would have a considerable impact upon the system. All of these structures should be dictated by the psychological considerations introduced earlier. For example, it may not be wise to use pure blue for important items as it is not easily noticed by human beings, nor a display that concentrated on red and green as some people are red–green colour blind. Neither would it be sensible to present complete circles and incomplete circles and expect the user to notice the difference. The effects of **closure** – the

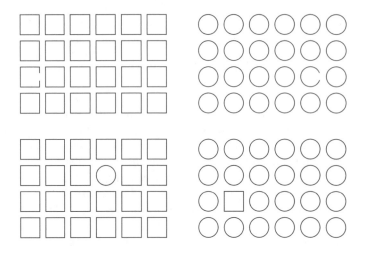

Figure 5.10 *The effects of closure*

tendency for human beings to complete incomplete figures – would undoubtedly interfere with the likelihood of the user performing successfully.
Figure 5.10 shows some examples. It would be more difficult to spot the
incomplete circle or square than to spot the circle amongst the squares or the
square amongst the circles.

The user is unlikely to remain static in terms of understanding and use of a
system. It is more likely that the inexperienced will gradually become more
experienced, or may stop using the system altogether. The intermittent user
might become a more frequent user or perhaps cease to use computers in their
work. Experts can also change. A computer system must, therefore, consider
the likelihood of change and take this on board. It might be that the particular
users of a system are always novices or always experts but the likelihood of this
occurring is perhaps not very great. For example, a university library will have
an influx of new users every year. It is much more likely that a range of ability
will be encountered by the designer of a system and will need to be provided
for.

5.7 Strategies for representing design

There are several methods for representing designs, either for the user to
examine prior to the development of the system or as a means of allowing the
design team to check the design, keep a record of the design or to evaluate the
design so far. There are specialist books on the subject so all that can be offered
here is a brief look at some of the more accessible strategies. The design tools
covered in this section are storyboards, state transition diagrams and rapid
prototyping using an interface builder.

Storyboards

The initial designs for the system can most conveniently be presented in the form of storyboards. At the simplest level the design team might sketch a design for the user to look at. This design might be very temporal in that it could be drawn and modified on a white board. However, when the design is beyond the embryonic stage and a little more concrete, it is useful to go to the user with a storyboard.

A storyboard consists of parts of the interface mounted onto card or paper. My own students at South Bank are encouraged to use either screen dumps produced from a drawing package or scale drawings. These are placed on the board and can be moved around by the user until a suitable and comfortable design emerges. We have found that users prefer to move paper around rather than point to elements on a screen which they cannot easily move round for themselves. A paper interface is a lot less intimidating than an on screen one. It does not require particular expertise to move paper about whereas an on screen prototype would require a usability engineer to make the changes for the user. This would mean that the user's ideas have to be properly interpreted and the user is not directly involved in the way that moving paper elements around on a card would encourage user involvement. Psychologically the user is more likely to suggest changes to a paper system rather than an on screen prototype.

The storyboard can be used in two ways. It can consist of mock ups of the screens with the various elements movable around each screen. Blu-tack can be used to hold the elements into place once the users are pleased with the finish appearance.

Secondly, the storyboard can be used to trace progression from one part of the screen to another and to check understanding of the various commands, dialogues etc.

The storyboard is a cheap and effective way of checking the design of the system in the very early stages. It is useful for the way in which it allows designers and end users to discuss the system together and to try out their various ideas. Figure 5.11 shows an example of a storyboard.

State transition diagrams

The state transition diagram is a means of representing the design. It can be used to ensure that all parts of the interface have been accounted for and it can be used as a means of checking potential user inputs and their outcomes. The STD is a vital tool to the developer of GUIs but it might be hard for a non-computer literate user to understand. However, some of my students have used a simplified STD and the storyboard to represent designs so that they are suitable for the user to look at. Figure 5.12 shows a state transition diagram.

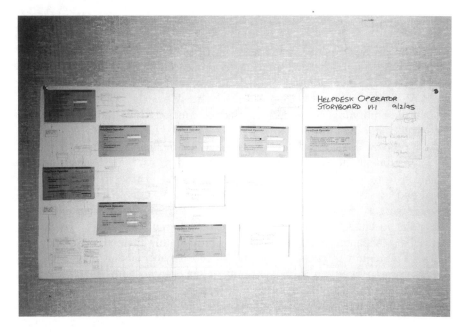

Figure 5.11 *A storyboard*

Rapid prototyping

Rapid prototyping is useful when the user is unsure what the system should be like, or is liable to lose interest, or is a novice user and the prototyping stage is intended to act as a means of training the users to a particular standard prior to the introduction of the finished product. Some software engineers frown on rapid prototyping as they believe it encourages sloppy habits. Rapid prototyping of the interface should be seen merely as a means of getting the design right. The system will still have to undergo the proper developmental process, will have to be designed from a programming point of view and must be properly represented at all stages otherwise it will become impossible to maintain.

Some programming environments are particular adept at being used for the rapid production of interfaces. Sadly, the ease at which these can be produced all too often causes the systems to be a mishmash of hacked together code which would be a nightmare to verify and to maintain (Culwin and Faulkner, 1997). Rapid prototyping must not be seen as a means of escaping a properly engineered product. If software is to be seen to be fit for its purpose then it must be properly documented and maintainable. It must be properly designed and code must not be written by the seat of the pants.

The rapid prototype allows the user to evaluate the system as it develops and user feedback can then be used in the further development of the system. This is known as the design, build, evaluate cycle (Ashworth, 1991). Figure 5.13 shows this process.

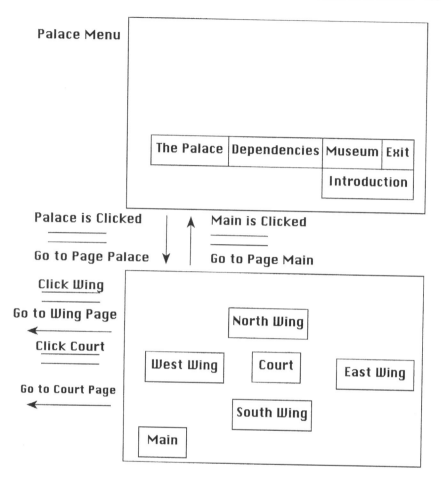

Palace Menu

The Palace	Dependencies	Museum	Exit
		Introduction	

Palace is Clicked

Go to Page Palace

Main is Clicked

Go to Page Main

Click Wing

Go to Wing Page

Click Court

Go to Court Page

North Wing

West Wing   Court   East Wing

South Wing

Main

Figure 5.12 *A state transition diagram*

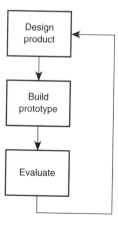

Figure 5.13 *Rapid prototyping using user feedback to drive the product*

5.13 Further reading

Dix, A. *et al.* (1997) *Human–Computer Interaction*, 2nd edn, Hemel Hempstead: Prentice Hall.
This has good sections on the design process and task analysis.

Eberts, R. E. (1994) *User Interface Design*, Englewood Cliffs, NJ: Prentice Hall.
This is good on task analysis.

Hix, D. and Hartson, H. (1993) *Developing User Interfaces*, Chichester: John Wiley.
Has excellent chapters on methods of representing design.

Shneiderman, B. (1992) *Designing the User Interface*, Reading, MA: Addison-Wesley.
Has a good chapter on user types and looks at some of the special needs.

CHAPTER 6

Evaluation and testing

Chapter overview

This chapter looks at evaluation from the point of view of its position in the development cycle. It also examines various methods of evaluating systems and discusses their strengths and weaknesses.

6.1 The importance of evaluation

Evaluation is relied on quite heavily by HCI. Because it remains difficult to design, it is hoped that evaluation will get rid of any problems that might be present in the systems. Although design techniques have improved and today HCI practitioners have a much better understanding of how they ought to go about the task of designing for others, evaluation remains very important. Evaluation is the parallel to systems testing in software engineering. It is the process by which the interface is tested against the needs and practices of the user. Just as in software engineering it is necessary to have a clear set of goals for the testing of software so it is in testing a system with the user. Therefore, it is important to decide what aspect of, when and how the user interface will be tested and by whom the testing will be done.

Methods of ensuring that the design team has a good understanding of what the user actually wants to do can be used. This takes some of the guess work out of design and can also offer a means of evaluating a system. Usability engineering is one such method of ensuring that a system is useful for the particular task it has been designed to perform. This will be examined in a later chapter.

Evaluation is inevitably going to bring design teams into contact with users and their attitudes. This means that as well as understanding when, where, why and how the systems will be evaluated, it will also be necessary to find ways of measuring attitudes and obtaining feedback from the users. These attitudes and findings must not be biased by the opinions and findings of the evaluation team themselves. It might be that members of the design team are not, therefore, involved directly in the evaluation of a given system. If the system's developer is part of a large organization then it may be possible that the evaluation of a particular design is carried out by a separate evaluation team, or by a different development team.

This chapter examines methods of evaluation and looks at some of the problems that can be encountered during the process of evaluating a system.

6.2 Problem areas in evaluation

The testing of the system, like the design process, is fraught with problems and difficulties. It is very easy to make mistakes or to test the wrong thing or the wrong person. There follows a list of relatively common problem areas in testing.

Common sense

It is tempting to assume that because something seems obvious it must be correct. However, the results of research often contradict what common sense might insist is true.

One of my favourite examples of common sense is in the design of the first generation of office chairs provided for programmers and other VDU users, by ergonomists. These were later found to be unsuitable since workers did not adopt the positions that common sense told ergonomists they would (Grand-jean, 1987). Grandjean compares the upright position the ergonomists favoured with the slumped position they actually adopted with the wry comment – 'wishful thinking' and 'reality'. It is best to try not to avoid making assumptions about anything.

Testing it on yourself

Testing a system on yourself is another dangerous mistake since the designer of a system can hardly be expected to be typical. The problem is that the designer as a designer has skills that the average person does not have and the design process will involve adding to those skills. Even if the designer starts off as a naive user of a computer system, the task of design will involve having to learn about the system and the lack of knowledge the task was started with will soon disappear.

Consulting the real end user

First of all, it has to be noted that it is easy to be told that this is what the task performer does. Design teams have to beware of this situation. The people in charge do not always know how a task is performed. The people in charge do know how they want the task done, or how it ought to be done, or how it used to be done. For a real understanding of what actually occurs you have to speak to the people performing the tasks. Design teams ignore real users at their peril! Task performers know what they do and the design team must speak them.

Secondly, the task performer may decide that the design team wants to be told how the task ought to be done, used to be done and so on. The team must ensure that they have the confidence of anyone providing information and there should be no recriminations.

Deciding when to change things

If a design team is asked to design a new system then there are two contradictory errors which might occur:

- Keeping things as they are because it has always be done in this way;
- Changing things because it is a new system

It is very important to look at the task and to decide what the best way to perform the task might be. This means that it is necessary to take into consideration the advantages of positive transfer as compared to the problems of learning a new system.

It is easier to build this way

It is easy to assume a solution because the technicalities pose a solution that is easiest to implement. It is important that human factors come first and that any sacrifice of ease of use for the benefit of implementation is done knowingly.

It can be evaluated later . . .

Evaluation needs to come early. Design decisions can be difficult to reverse if evaluation appears late. It should be seen as an on-going process: design – evaluate – redesign.

Evaluation carried out on the wrong people

The evaluation of the system must be done on a representative group. Many of the design problems we now face in every day life have been caused by the testing of systems on people who know too much about the system in the first place or are themselves designers.

The complicated interfaces to some household equipment, for example, are the results of designs being incremental and then testing being carried out on the team that did the designing (Thimbleby, 1991). Obviously, it is easier to add to knowledge already obtained than it is to start from scratch. All too often, testing is not carried out on someone who has to start from scratch. Thus design teams are unaware of the burden being placed on the end user of a particular system.

6.3 When and what to evaluate

Ideally, any testing carried out by the design team should be in circumstances identical or very close to the real conditions the system will be operating in. If it is possible for the system to be tested where it is to be used, then obviously there should be a preference for that. As a design passes through the stages and finally becomes a finished product, so the cost of rectifying errors in the design increases. It is therefore of paramount importance to test at the early stages. It is in everyone's interest to ensure that the final testing confirms earlier design and brings to light only the most minor of problems.

The following stages represent points at which testing can/should take place. At each stage, recommendations about what to look for, the cost of redesigning and so on will be commented upon.

Systems analysis phase

Where possible, the interface designer should analyze work that has been done in similar fields. This way it will be possible to get feedback from users of previously designed systems. This feedback can then be used to produce scenarios and consider feasibility.

Obviously, it is more economic to use work that has already been done as a basis for the new design, rather than starting from scratch. However, it will not always be possible to do that. At this stage changes to the system or the abandonment of the proposal are at their cheapest.

System design phase

Parts of the system can be simulated and tested during the design stage. The prototypes need not be working systems, they can be mock ups, parts of systems, paper systems, systems built using a prototyping tool, storyboards. These are relatively cheap to produce so the advantages of different types of design can be measured against each other at this stage.

Although it is tempting to get on with the production of the system, it is much easier to make changes at this early stage rather than later. If a modular approach is taken to design, the cost of making changes is again reduced. These designs ought to be taken seriously though. A prototype does not necessarily imply something that will be thrown away, although some prototypes are designed as throwaways. The fewer alterations that need to be made, the smaller the final cost. Prototypes are a serious business and should therefore be treated as such. It is not the case that design–evaluate–redesign means not designing seriously.

Pre-production phase

When the prototype is complete, evaluation can take place on a larger scale and can concentrate on the details of the system. There are many ways of measuring user performance with a system and these can be used at this stage to evaluate the different aspects of the design. A later chapter will examine usability engineering since this will offer a structure that allows the design team and the user to have more confidence in the effectiveness of the particular design.

6.4 Evaluation techniques

Basically, there are two quite different approaches that can be adopted in the evaluation of a system. However, it is also possible to combine the two techniques. The first method is the *analytic evaluation* method and consists of a formal pencil and paper evaluation of tasks and goal – for example, the GOMS methodology suggest by Card *et al.* (1983).

The second method is the *empirical method* and consists of an analysis of user performance in relation to the proposed system. It might consist of tasks to be performed with the system, observation, questionnaires, experiments and interviews.

6.5 Experiments

There are two basic approaches to experimentation on the users of a new system. You can test the new system's performance in relation to an existing system – *comparative experiments* or the new system can be tested in isolation – *absolute experiments*.

Techniques for the design of the interface can vary from the formal to the informal. The more formal methods – experiments, for example – tend to be expensive because they require controlled environments and skilled personnel to administer them.

Experimental method

Because psychology wishes to be taken seriously as a science it uses a set of procedures to establish scientific facts. This means that a cause and effect relationship has been established through experiment. In order to go about this task, the following must be adhered to:

1 identify the problem and formulate hypothetical cause and effect relations among variables;
2 design and execute the experiment;
3 examine data from the experiment;
4 communicate the results.

Before the experiment can be carried out the research question has to be formulated. The research question will direct the research and experimentation so it needs to be chosen with care. The experiment will be designed on the basis of the hypothesis formation and the independent and dependent variables will emerge from this. At the same time, the target group will be identified.

Hypothesis formation

The experiment is the most rigorous method of testing a hypothesis. It involves the researcher testing out ideas in a controlled environment and setting the conditions to cause particular effects to happen.

A hypothesis is a prediction about what will happen given a particular situation. For example, the following might be a suitable *experimental hypothesis*:

'Users of a word processing system learn faster when they are given feedback.'

At the same time a **null hypothesis** is formulated. The experimental hypothesis predicts that the independent variable is affected by the dependent variable. The null hypothesis predicts that the independent variable will not be affected by the dependent variable. The null hypothesis for this experiment would be:

'There will be no difference between users given feedback and those not given feedback.'

Once the hypothesis has been formed then it is necessary to set up some sort of study to test whether it is true or not.

The experimental methods shows that only one factor can account for a given observed effect. That means that all other factors have to be discounted by careful control of the experiment. The factor that is being observed is known as the **dependent variable**. All other factors that are being discounted are known as the extraneous factors. These may be discounted through careful experiment design or by showing that the cause and effect relationship between

Figure 6.1 *The relationship between independent and dependent variables*

the independent variable and the observed behaviour still holds true when these other factors are controlled, eliminated or in some way manipulated. The factor that is being manipulated is called the **independent variable**. See Figure 6.1.

In this example the important factor that has been isolated is feedback. This is what will affect the user's ability to learn the system. This is the independent variable and it is something that is set up by the evaluation team to see if it is affecting a person's behaviour in some specific way. Here, the behaviour is the user's performance in acquiring knowledge of the word processing system – this is the dependent variable. The dependent variable is measured to see if it is influenced by the independent variable.

Of course, this sounds very simple and the process is not quite that easy. For example, it might not be that feedback affected the users but something else did. It is therefore necessary to ensure that the improvement really is the result of the feedback and nothing else.

Problems and solutions

One of the ways to ensure that the independent variable is responsible for any improvement in behaviour is by using **control groups**. This method uses two groups of subjects; the first group is given feedback and the second none. It is hoped this means that it can be deduced how users would have performed if they were not given any feedback at all, and then that performance can be compared with the performance of the group that is given feedback. Providing that no other influences came into play, the only difference between the groups would be the independent variable – feedback. The **control group** is the group which is used to make the comparison and the **experimental group** is the group that experiences the independent variable.

There is still a problem because it may be that one group of people has accidentally been chosen in such a way that they are for some reason already better at doing the tasks set. The evaluation team has to make sure that the groups are the same so far as their composition is concerned and they can do that by making sure that the groups are the same. This process is known as **matching** and it can give problems! It means that particular attributes have to be identified and must be present in both groups. In the example of the feedback question it might be necessary to ensure that both groups cover particular numbers of men and women and age groups and occupations. If the groups are not matched and the experimental group performs better it would be difficult to say what had caused that better performance. Problems like this are called **confounding variables** because they are things that can upset the findings.

However, it might not be possible or desirable to have two groups and the evaluation team may decide that they want to control the variables in some other way. For example, they might decide to give each user a period of time with the system when they were not given feedback and then give them some time when they were. The results from each experiment could then be compared. In this case the performance of each individual would be compared with that individual's own performance and it could be assumed that individual differences had been controlled (or would they?). This type of experimental design is called **repeated measures design** whereas when different people undergo each condition of the independent variable this is called **independent measures design**.

There are still some remaining problems, however. Sometimes performance can be affected by the order in which things are presented to the subjects – **the order effect**. The effect of practice, **the practice effect**, has to be ruled out. This is a problem that occurs in many different psychological tests and has been evident in memory experiments. The subject simply gets better at the task as the task is repeated. On the other hand, it is possible that subjects may become tired and do worse as the experiment progresses, **the fatigue effect**. These order effects can be controlled by **counterbalancing**. This is a process by which one half of the subjects do one condition of the independent variable first and the other do the other condition of the independent variable first. For example, one half of the subjects would receive feedback first while the other received no feedback. The final results will show the whole scores so any effects should have been cancelled out because they will have affected the two conditions of the independent variable equally.

The whole point of experimental design is to control as many aspects of the process as possible. In the example examined here the evaluation team has to ensure that nothing other than the independent variable is affecting the user's performance. This means ruling out any environmental factors that might possibly influence the result. For example, if the room in which the experiment was carried out on one group was noisy this might affect the results.

Finally, anyone who is involved in evaluating a system has to remember that they are working with people, not objects, and will need to take care that they do not do anything that might cause the subjects harm emotionally, physically or psychologically. Experiments have to be thought out with care and the team needs to make sure that there are no adverse effects upon the subjects. For example, it would be unacceptable to design an experiment in which the user is punished for making an error in the use of a system. Whenever people are used to test systems, it would be wise to carry out the following:

- explain to the subject what is expected;
- explain that the subject is free to leave or quit the experiment at any time;
- explain what the purpose of the experiment is;
- make sure that the subject is comfortable;
- explain that the results are confidential and how they will be used;
- where possible get the subject to agree, in writing, to the guidelines you have set.

Never at any time do anything to embarrass, hurt or otherwise distress the subject.

6.6 Questionnaires

The advantage of a questionnaire is that once produced it can provide a vast body of information. However, the production of a good questionnaire is time consuming and if it is to be done correctly, it requires several stages. Any questionnaire should go through the design–evaluate–redesign cycle until the evaluators are certain that the responses will be the sort of responses they want and the questionnaire will be understood in the same way, by those filling in the answers.

It has also to be remembered that the questionnaires have to be examined after they have been collected and the findings have to be analyzed. This can be very time consuming so it is important to ensure that the questionnaire design starts off with a suitable hypothesis or research question and no questions are asked about subjects that the evaluator does not need to know about. It is also important to ensure that the questionnaire is easy to analyze.

Questionnaires are a good source of attitude measurement.

Questionnaires can be either **interviewer administered** or **self-administered**. The advantages and disadvantages of each method will be discussed below.

Questions can be **open** or **closed**. Open questions are good for gaining information on a broad basis because they allow the respondents to answer in any way they choose. For example, an open question might be:

'What aspects of the interface did you like most?'

The closed question is limited and the responses are chosen from a given list. For example, a closed question based on the example above would be:

'Which aspects of the interface did you like most?'
(a) the colours; (b) the sound; (c) the ease of moving from area to area.

The problem with open questions is that they can produce too much data which is not easily analysed because it is so diverse. However, closed questions can distort findings simply because they suggest things to people that might not otherwise occur to them.

Interviewer administered questionnaires

This implies the existence and availability of interviewers trained in the technique. It requires a considerable amount of time to carry out but it has the advantage that the gathering of data is controlled by the interviewer. Also, if there are difficulties over understanding, the interviewer can clarify what is necessary in the answer.

Self-administered questionnaires

These require fewer person hours to deliver but there are several problems that can occur:

- there is poor control over returns;
- questions cannot be explained by the interviewer so they have to be carefully written;
- there is a high likelihood of bias because of the small number of responses.

Problems in questionnaire design

Wording of suitable questions for a questionnaire is not simple and there are many places where problems can occur.

1 *Use of loaded terms.* It is important not to bias the reply by using emotionally significant terms.
2 *Suggesting the desired response.* For example: 'You have stopped beating your dog, haven't you?' is difficult to answer without implying some fault in the first place. Questions need to be in a neutral tone and should not be phrased in such a way that the person is likely to answer yes. If you use the "You do ... don't you?" structure then this is likely to lead to answers consisting of yes or no.

   I was once shown a professionally designed questionnaire which had the question Do you wash fruit and vegetables before putting them away, before use or never wash them. I guess very few people would admit to not washing!

3 *Embarrassing the subject.* This can arise where the subject feels, for example, that the answer implies some inadequacy on the part of the subject. For example, a long list of applications which subjects are asked to tick if they are acquainted with them may make a user who has none or very few to tick feel inferior. Some subjects will tick

applications they do not know simply because they think it looks better if they do.

> Some of my students carried out a survey on icons. Their first question was 'Can you identify the following icons?' Unfortunately, the respondents took that as a test of their ability rather than as a criticism of the icons.

4   *Lack of precision in questions leading to imprecise answers.* Avoid questions that give answers like 'seldom', 'frequently', 'often'. It will be unclear to the subject just what these terms mean as they are far too subjective.

> Imprecision can mean more than is obvious. Again, a group of computing students carrying out a survey asked: "What is your first language?" They were expecting replies like English, French, Chinese etc., instead they got C++ and Ada.

6.7 Recommendations for questionnaire design

1   Closed questions are better than open questions. There can always be a 'don't know' reply if necessary.
2   Questions need to be structured carefully, and should progress from the general to the detailed. The first questions should be neutral and easily answered. More sensitive questions should be left until later in the questionnaire. It is important to order questions carefully and thus to avoid **forward-referencing** where one answer prepares the subject for a question which is asked later on or **sequence bias** where one question influences the next answer.
3   Questionnaires must not be too long (two sides of A4 is quite enough). Filter questions can be used to allow answers to questions to be ignored. For example, a person who is hard of hearing might have quite different television viewing habits, from someone with average hearing. Branch questions can also be used to allow subjects to ignore questions. For example:

'Do you own a word processing package?'

could be used to allow the subject to branch to a different part of the questionnaire.
4   The questionnaire must be attractive so that it will appeal to the subject.
5   It is also very important to try the questionnaire out first prior to its actual use. This will allow the team to find out what difficulties might arise in providing answers, or where answers might be ambiguous.

6.8 Questionnaire types

Multi choice questions and checklists

The simplest form of questionnaire might ask the user for a yes/no response. Some questionnaires add a don't know/don't have an opinion category. See Figure 6.2.

Checklists are also useful. These might gather information about what systems a user has used or what aspects of a system have been used. See Figure 6.3. More complex multichoice questionnaires can be built up from these simple beginnings, but they are usually more like complex checklists.

Scalar questionnaire

A **scalar questionnaire** asks the subject to register an opinion based on a pre-defined scale. These scales have numerical values attached to them or a linguistic scale. See Figure 6.4.

```
Have you used MagicDraw before?
                    yes            no         don't know
```

Figure 6.2 *Simple yes/no questionnaire*

```
Which of the following commands did you use? Tick all that
apply.
                yes        no        not sure
Paste
Cut
Clear
Copy
```

Figure 6.3 *A checklist*

Rate the usefulness of the e-mail system

Very useful   Not useful

Figure 6.4 *A multi point rating scale*

The new e-mail system is very effective

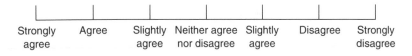

| Strongly agree | Agree | Slightly agree | Neither agree nor disagree | Slightly agree | Disagree | Strongly disagree |

Figure 6.5 *A Likert scale*

Some questionnaire designers deliberately miss out a middle category from questions like this in order to force the respondent into an opinion either way. A middle category is very much like adding a 'don't know/don't have an opinion' category to a question and when this is present some 10–40 per cent of respondents will shift their answer to that section (Plous, 1993). Questions without middle categories are good for collecting general opinions and they avoid the disadvantage of allowing people to sit on the fence. The disadvantage of using no middle category is that it does force people to decide between opinions they may not really have strong feelings about and it may cause them to register arficial opinions.

A Likert scale is a scalar questionnaire where the strength of opinion is gathered as in Figure 6.5.

A **semantic differential scale** uses antonyms to represent two opposing views. The scales between these views are then given usually with a neutral view in the middle, as in Figure 6.6.

Rate the e-mail system on the following criteria.

	Very	Quite	Neutral	Quite	Very	
Easy						Hard
Useful						Useless
Fun						Tedious
Fast						Slow

Figure 6.6 *A semantic differential scale*

Place the following packages in order of usefulness. Use a scale of 1 to 4 with 1 being the most useful and 4 being the least useful.

MagicDraw ☐   AccuSpell ☐

QuickRite ☐   GrammaFix ☐

Figure 6.7 *A ranked order questionnaire*

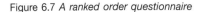

A **ranked order questionnaire** asks the respondents to rank their opinions. Figure 6.7 gives an example.

6.9 Interviews

Any of the evaluation methods could be used as a method of first gathering information about an existing system. It is important that the design team gets the confidence of the end users and involves them in the design process. They should not be passive providers of information but active participants in the design process, that way they will get a system they want and need rather than a system that the design team thinks they want and need.

It is important to remember that unstructured interviews, like open questions, can be difficult to analyze.

6.10 Observation

It is useful to watch the performers of a task do the task. Particularly if they can be persuaded to ignore the evaluators and perhaps to vocalise what is being done. It is important not to disturb the way in which an individual works on a task nor must any extraneous conditions or tools be imposed upon them. It is important to ensure that any user who agrees to be observed is happy about that and that the users are doing what it is that they really do. If the evaluation team has the confidence of the users the users are less likely to be disturbed.

It is important to remember that people being watched can act in a different way because of the presence of the observer. This is called the **Hawthorne effect**, named after a study carried out at the Hawthorne electrical assembly works in Chicago in the 1920s. The aim of the study was to examine the effect of lighting upon work. However, it became obvious that the study was being affected by extraneous factors since at one point productivity increased steadily as lighting levels were reduced to the point where workers complained that they could no longer see!

Figure 6.8 shows HCI students at South Bank University working with users who are testing software products.

The Wizard of Oz is a variation where one of the evaluation team acts as part of the system, for example a voice or a system which feeds back to a screen. The users think they are working with a real system but really it is a member of the team either typing back to the screen or acting as the output verbally. Obviously, the 'wizard' is hidden from the user's view. This enables direct watching of the user at the time and the team can respond in real time. It enables a system to be tested in the very early stages and cheaply since the real system does not have to be built. It also enables the team to watch very closely what the user is doing.

Figure 6.8 *Observation*

Eberts (1994) notes that the technique was designed for testing natural language interfaces, presumably because of the difficulties of building the real thing. But there is no reason that the method could not be used elsewhere.

6.11 Activity sampling and activity logging

The tasks are sampled or logged, or both. This can be done by either a member of the design team or the performer of the task or by the system itself. When done by the task performer it can interfere with the way in which a task is performed so the evaluator needs to remember that.

Some laboratories use videos as a method of recording what the user does. Recording the user by video, if done openly, can interfere with the user's performance. Secret recording of the user may incur the wrath of a user, and understandably so. Many HCI practitioners are not happy with the idea of secretly recording behaviour. Activity logging when done by the system seems to be easier for users to ignore.

Norman has also raised the question as to whether the various recordings that people make ever get replayed as it takes much longer to watch or listen to a recording than it does to watch the event in the first place (Norman, 1992). Some laboratories watch the user during recording and then make notes so they can return to points in the video. If recording is to take place, this seems a good way to make the process useful.

6.12 Co-operative evaluation

Andrew Monk and his team at the University of York have designed a method by which the user is encouraged to talk to the evaluator (Monk *et al.*, 1993). This is called co-operative evaluation because it implies that the designer and the user work together over the interface and discuss the problems as and when they arise. Monk envisages that this will occur at the very early stages of the design before the system is properly built. It can actually be used at any stage though and works well on parts of the system and even on paper prototypes. The user is encouraged to talk aloud and to say why certain actions are being done. Co-operative evaluation can be used in conjunction with questionnaires but it does need a sensible task list in order to work effectively.

My own HCI students use this method and variations on it and find it easy to learn and to carry out and very rewarding from both the point of view of the evaluator and the subject.

6.13 Summary

Evaluation is an important part of HCI because it hopes to eradicate any problems that may be present in a system. Furthermore it is the process by which HCI practitioners can learn about what users think and what makes a good system.

Evaluation is the parallel to systems testing in software engineering and allows the system to be judged against the requirements of the user.

Evaluation brings the design team into contact with the user and care must be taken that the subjects used in any evaluation exercise are happy about the part they will be playing.

There are many problems in the evaluation of a system and the design team has to ensure that these are minimized by the careful design of the evaluation methods. Evaluations should start with a research question however informal the testing ends up being.

Although the system may be tested on the design team, it has to be remembered that at some stage real users have to be exposed to the product and however well meaning the design team is, it cannot substitute for real subjects.

The evaluation of a system should be carried out as soon as possible. The later the evaluation is left the more costly it will be to rectify mistakes.

Evaluation methods can be divided into formal and informal methods. Both methods have their place in the evaluation of the system and either may be used at the various stages of the development of the system.

6.14 Self test list

absolute experiments
analytic evaluation
checklists
closed questions
comparative experiments
control group
co-operative evaluation
counterbalancing
dependent variable
empirical method
experimental group
experimental hypothesis
fatigue effect
forward referencing
Hawthorne effect
independent variable
interviewer administered questionnaires
Likert scale
matching
multi choice questions
multi point rating scale
null hypothesis
open questions
order effect
practice effect
self administered questionnaires
semantic differential scale
sequence bias
Wizard of Oz

6.15 Exercises

1   Collect a number of questionnaires and look at them carefully. Decide
    which you like most and which least. Try to work out what you think
    the questionnaire's aim might be.
2   What problems would you have with gathering opinions about computer
    systems?
3   How can you use evaluation to correct faults in the system? How can
    you be certain that your evaluation of a system is accurate?

4 What problems might there be in involving users in the process of building systems? How can you cope with these problems?

5 A word processing package uses two different colour schemes. One is a blue background with yellow text and the other is a red background with green text. It is necessary to test the system to find out which colour scheme is best.

Produce a suitable test question for the above scenario. Using the test question design a suitable experiment. Explain exactly what you would do, how you would carry out the experiment and what you would hope to discover with the results. What problems there might be?

1. Rate the usefulness of the e-mail system

Very useful   Not useful

2. What is your academic background?

Arts ☐   Science ☐

Social Sciences ☐   Technical ☐

3. I write long e-mail messages

Strongly   Agree   Slightly   Neither agree   Slightly   Disagree   Strongly
agree   agree   nor disagree   agree   disagree

4. Which gender are you?

Female ☐   Male ☐

5. Tick your age group

16 to 21 ☐   22 to 30 ☐

31 to 35 ☐   36 to 70 ☐

Figure 6.9 *A questionnaire about e-mail*

6 How else could the above system be tested and what advantages if any would you get from the alternate method?

7 Figure 6.9 shows a questionnaire. What do you think the hypothesis behind this questionnaire might be? Produce a suitable hypothesis and modify the questionnaire to improve it.

8 It is necessary to gather opinions about how easy it is to use a word processing system. The survey wishes to find out how much the users like the new system in relationship with the old one. How would you prefer to gather opinions about this system? Explain your reasons.

6.16 References

Card, S. *et al.* (1983) *The Psychology of Human–Computer Interaction*, New Jersey: Lawrence Erlbaum Associates.

Grandjean, E. (1987) *Ergonomics in Computerised Offices*, London: Taylor and Francis.

Monk, A. *et al.* (1993) *Improving Your Human Computer Interface*, New York: Prentice Hall.

Norman, D. (1992) *Turn Signals Are the Facial Expressions of Automobiles*, Reading, MA: Addison–Wesley.

Plous, S. (1993) *The Psychology of Judgment and Decision Making*, New York: McGraw–Hill.

Thimbleby, H. (1991) 'Can anyone work the video?' *New Scientist*, 23rd February, 48–51.

6.17 Further reading

Coolican, H. (1995) *Research Methods and Statistics in Psychology*. London: Hodder and Stoughton.

This is aimed at psychology students so the text can be skimmed where necessary although I found it a good read and very entertaining. He has some good short exercises and answers at the back to make you feel good! He covers questionnaire design too.

Eberts, R. (1994) *User Interface Design*, Englewood Cliffs, NJ: Prentice Hall.

Eberts has good sections on evaluation and covers in some detail the Wizard of Oz method. He has examples of how it was used. He also examines the analytical methods like GOMS.

Harris, P. (1986) *Designing and Reporting Experiments*, Milton Keynes: Open University Press.

Another book aimed at psychology students but there are some good tips and excellent examples.

Lisney, M. (1989) *Psychology Experiments, Investigations and Practicals*, Oxford: Blackwell.

Provides a more detailed description of experimental method and some good exercises. It is highly readable, more like a detective novel than a text book but very thorough and kindly. It deals with experimental design in some detail and looks at statistical analysis. It is a good starting point for those readers who want to examine experiments in more depth but would like a gentle approach.

Monk, A. *et al.* (1993) *Improving Your Human Computer Interface*, New York: Prentice Hall.
Provides an excellent description of the process of co-operative evaluation, has worked examples and an example for the reader to try. The book is also easy to read and thought provoking.

Plous, S. (1993) *The Psychology of Judgment and Decision Making*, New York: McGraw–Hill.
This is an excellent and entertaining description of how people make decisions. He has interesting things to say about questionnaire design.

Robson, C. (1990) *Experiment, Design and Statistics in Psychology*, 2nd edn, London: Penguin.
Again, this is very readable and chatty but more advanced than the Lisney book.

Tognazzini, B. (1992) *Tog on the Interface*, Reading, MA: Addison–Wesley.
Has some useful and amusing things to say about user testing. He shows how testing can be done very cheaply. This book is well worth reading for his examples and stories.

CHAPTER 7
Making systems that people can use

Chapter overview

This chapter looks at ways to ensure that the finished system is what the user wants. It introduces the concept of usability engineering and offers some guidelines for the development of systems that will fulfil the user's needs.

7.1 Usability engineering

One of the biggest problems the designers of a human–computer system face is ensuring that the finished product is what the user really wants and needs. It is no simple task to ensure that a product is fit for the purpose it was designed for when the purpose is as complicated as many computer systems are endeavouring to fulfil. The problem is knowing exactly what sort of system that the user wants and producing the best system for that particular task and that particular user.

Usability engineering endeavours to solve this problem of ensuring that the system is fit for the purpose for which it was designed. One of the ways in which it is able to operate is by evaluating the system so that any deficiencies are designed out. To evaluate a system effectively it might be useful to have criteria to measure the system against. The ideal situation would be to design the system to fulfil the needs of the user. The system could then be evaluated in terms of this list of requirements and this would also make the process of testing much easier. This process would mean that what the user receives is a truly usable system. This method of producing software is known as *usability engineering*.

Usability is a concept that has emerged from the ergonomics side of HCI. While the design process remains difficult, HCI leans heavily upon evaluation and usability is a facet of evaluation that allows the development team to measure the interface against criteria that have been selected. Usability is not exclusive to HCI and the techniques available to HCI experts have been around in ergonomics for some time. Usability addresses the practical rather than the heavily theoretical. Usability engineering looks at real users in action and measures the system in terms of a pre-defined set of criteria.

Objectives in usability engineering

Ensuring that a product is usable is not easy. Guaranteeing that usability is even more problematic. Usability engineering helps to solve the problem of designing something that the user really wants and will actually use. It does this by:

- defining usability through metrics;
- setting planned levels for usability attributes;
- incorporating user-derived feedback into the design process;
- repeating all of the above until usability levels are met or amended by agreement with the user.

The aims of usability engineering

All decisions about the usability of the interface should always be made by the designer. These will be conscious and explicit and the designer will know the reasons for them since they will have been made consciously. However, not all decisions are made like this and some will be hidden, or unconscious and implicit. To avoid the latter it is important that goals are visible, and effective collaboration between members of the design team is supported. In this way, when design decisions are made the design team is in control of them. Decisions are not made by default or unconsciously. The idea of usability engineering is to help to make this process of design open and apparent and to have ways of measuring that result against criteria that have been agreed on well in advance.

7.2 Defining objectives in usability engineering

The aim of the usability approach is to identify what success is and decide how it might be measured. Obviously, this will involve the recognition and adoption of a series of attributes that are measurable. For example, it might be decided that the following are a good list of attributes for a particular piece of software. This list can subsequently be used to measure the success of the application. For example, it might consist of:

- learnability
- throughput
- user satisfaction

Learnability

Quite clearly a system will require some amount of time for a user to learn how to use it even if this time is minimal. But other things can be measured as well. For example, it might be decided that the learnability of a particular application is best measured by examining all or some of the following criteria:

- the time required to learn the system;
- the time required to achieve a stated performance criterion;
- the difficulties observed in acquiring the necessary skill;
- user comments, suggestions and preferences

The measurement of learnability will also involve an objective measurement of just how easy the system is to learn. The following would make acceptable objective indicators, though, again, it might be necessary for the team to add others as required:

- the frequency of error messages;
- the frequency of particular error messages;
- the frequency of use of on-line help;
- the number of times the user needed help on a specific problem.

Throughput

Throughput is defined as the ease and efficiency of a system's use after the initial learning period. To examine the ease and efficiency of use the following criteria could be examined and measured:

- the time required to perform selected tasks;
- the success to failure rate in completing task;
- the frequency of use of various commands or of particular language features/functions;
- the time spent looking for information in documentation;
- the time spent using on-line help;
- the measurements of user problems as for learning;
- user comments, suggestions and preferences.

User satisfaction

It might seem unlikely that it would be possible to measure the satisfaction a user feels whilst using a system. Such a measurement would seem to be too subjective. However, a useful measurement of user satisfaction can be made if the evaluation team's measurement is based on observations of user attitudes towards the system.

The aim in designing the system is to promote continued and enhanced use of the system by the user. Thus the aim of usability engineering is to ensure that the user has positive feelings towards the system. It is possible to measure user attitudes using a questionnaire, for example:

How would you rate your overall opinion of the system?
1 = very bad to 5 = very good

It might be sensible to specify in advance that the aim is to achieve a user response of at least 90 per cent of users responding with scores of 4 or 5. In this

Table 7.1 *Usability specification*

Attribute:	Ease of throughput
Metric:	Error count
User set:	All users
Pre-conditions:	Measurement taken after 1 week of use

way, it is possible to provide a reasonably objective measurement of what else would be a very subjective response.

7.3 Usability engineering as a process

To produce an application using the usability engineering approach it is necessary to first produce a *usability specification* (see Table 7.1). This is a statement of usability attributes that will be examined. It states:

- how the criteria will be measured;
- what the criteria for representing the attainment is;
- which set or subset of users it applies to;
- what the pre-conditions for measurement are.

This specification will then be used as a basis for the evaluation of the application. The process of evaluation, redesign and re-evaluation can then be carried out until the required levels are met.

7.4 Extensions to the usability specification

Whiteside *et al.* (1988) have suggested that the usability specification should be expanded in order to specify performance criteria such as:

Worst case. This is the worst possible scenario for the system and one that will make it unacceptable.
Lowest acceptable level. This is the lowest level of performance that is acceptable by the user.
Planned case. This is the level that the system is expected to achieve.
Best case. This is the best possible scenario.
Now level. This is the current state of the system.

This would seem to be a very useful addition since it allows the application to be measured against a scale. It might be that this will make the task of evaluating between various systems much easier since real measurements can be put on the attributes and these compared. Also, it is much easier to set levels and make comparisons before development starts. The temptation is, that once a system is developed its level of performance becomes what was expected. Table 7.2 shows an example of this extended specification.

Table 7.2 *Extended usability specification*

Worst case:	More errors than at present
Lowest acceptable level:	Same errors as at present
Planned case:	Two errors every hour
Best case:	Error free performance
Now level:	Six errors per hour

7.5 Checklist for developing a usability specification

To carry out the measurements required by the usability approach, a suitable checklist is required. This might consist of the following:

- the time taken to complete the task;
- percentage of the task completed;
- percentage of the task completed per unit of time;
- ratio of success to failure;
- the time spent dealing with errors;
- the frequency of use of on-line help and documentation;
- the amount of time spent using help and documentation;
- the percentage of favourable/unfavourable user comments;
- the number of repetitions or failed commands;
- the number of good features recalled by user;
- the number of commands not used.

This checklist would be worked through and then the results could be compared with the expectations which have already been specified in the usability specification.

7.6 Usability metrics

Usability engineering requires that the users perform the task or tasks. This performance has to be evaluated and this can be done in a number of ways.

First, the user could perform the task. The evaluation team can then measure the performance in terms of the checklist given above. For example, the evaluation team can measure how much time was taken, how many errors were made or how much help was needed before the task was completed.

Secondly, it is possible to monitor users during evaluation trials, when they are using the system. This allows observation of difficulties encountered and how they are solved. This monitoring can be done in any of the ways suggested in the previous chapter.

Thirdly, the evaluation team can carry out interviews and obtain the necessary material that way. This might be a good way of obtaining information about user satisfaction with the system. A similar approach is to use questionnaires.

7.7 Socio-technical design

The aim of socio-technical design is to fit the process of design into the framework of the needs of the organization. Socio-technical design takes the idea of designing for the user and the task a stage further and endeavours to design within the structure of the organization and the way in which it operates. This finished product is more closely associated with and more suited to the needs of the organization. The social aspects of the organization are very important and need to be considered if truly effective systems are to be designed and built. Furthermore, socio-technical design takes into account the work done by the organization, its social composition and structure and the way in which it organizes itself. All of this implies that the end user is encouraged to have a significant part in the development of the system. Also, because the design of the system is concerned with the structure of the organization and its need, there is much more likelihood that it might be necessary for the development of a system to consider change.

Socio-technical design principles

The principles of socio-technical design are concerned with providing a framework for the production of applications which are truly in tune with the organization and the users who are using that system. To this end, the process of socio-technical design will turn its attention to those areas of concern. The following have been identified by the Tavistock Institute as important in the process of designing effectively for particular environments (Mumford and Sutton, 1991). The Tavistock Institute was formed in 1946 by a group of psychologists and others concerned with mental health and development of the individual.

Compatibility
The design process must be compatible with its objectives. The objectives need to be compatible with the work of the organization. End users will need to be involved in this process.

Minimum critical specifications
The specification will be drawn up to take into account the minimal needs of the organization. This specification should include everything which is essential but nothing unnecessary. Unnecessary functionality simply clutters a system and makes it over-complicated and therefore difficult to learn. If extra functionality might be needed at a later stage then it can always be hidden as in the case of short menus.

Socio-technical criterion
A problem should be controlled as closely as possible to the site of its origin. Problems that are passed on to be solved by someone else are problems that

will increase in size. Where the problem occurs is where the best understanding of the problem is likely to exist. Although others might be consulted, the problem is seen as belonging to the place it originated in. This gives the individuals concerned with it feelings of responsibility and control too and will increase their sense of self worth.

Multifunction

Employees should not be expected to perform fractions of tasks as this reduces job satisfaction and does not allow them to see their task through to the end. The work of Frederick Winslow Taylor led to the development of what was later known as **Taylorism**. This is the idea that workers should be given one discrete task. For example, one of my students explained to me once how he was part of a team making ham sandwiches. His task was to place the ham on the already buttered bread. Although there has been a tendency for Taylorism to dictate the construction of tasks in the past as fractions of larger tasks, socio-technical design seeks to place workers in control of processes and it accepts that partial tasks are unfulfilling for the individual. People take pride and pleasure in work that makes sense and an organization whose workers are content is much more likely to be successful. Socio-technical design concerns itself with the design of suitable tasks that will give the worker the sense of seeing the task through to the end.

Boundary location

The work boundaries separating one group from another must be chosen carefully. It is important that tasks are seen as being entire. It is also important that groups see themselves as groups and quite distinct from any other groups. Socio-technical design seeks to foster a sense of unity.

Information flow

Information should go to the place where it is used. It should not involve others as this can over-complicate a process and lead to error.

Support congruence

Systems should reinforce the behaviour of the organization. The nature of the organization should dictate the structure of the system and not the other way round.

Design and human values

Human–computer system design should concentrate on providing a high quality of working life for the people it is concerned with. This is seen as of paramount importance in socio-technical design. The quality of working life is important since if an individual feels happy and content the quality of work produced will be higher. Also, there is less chance of absenteeism, high personnel turnover and error.

The principle of incompletion
Design is iterative and continuous; design, evaluate, redesign.

Recommendations

1   Systems should support users in their tasks. They should be easy to learn, easy to use and easy to understand.
2   Systems should provide all information a user needs in an acceptable form. The user should not be expected to change work practices to fit in with a system.
3   People do more than one task at a time as a matter of course; this is known as multiple activities. They frequently prefer to operate in this way but it can lead to error, so systems should support scheduling and multi-tasking and make this easy.
4   People work in groups. Systems need to develop organizational interfaces in order to reflect the nature and work of the group using that particular interface.

Bjorn-Andersen (1985) has taken this a stage further and has suggested that designers should be developing systems that liberate the intellectual capabilities of the users. He suggests that this means developing systems that:

Do not monitor users. Where systems examine the work done by users either in terms of quality or amount of work done in a measured amount of time, the energies of the user will as a matter of course be directed against the system. The user will attempt to bypass the monitoring rather than do the work that is supposed to be done.
Are not condescending. Users quite rightly dislike being treated as if they are stupid. The system should treat them as equals. That is not the same as being complex. If an individual is involved in the training of someone else then the instructor does not adopt a condescending tone. The instructor talks at the same level, but in an explanatory way. A human–computer system should operate in the same way.
Leave as much responsibility as possible to the discretion of the user. Systems should not take away the user's right to decide. A system that does that will inevitably lead to the user developing low self-esteem. Inevitably, this will lead to dissatisfaction. The users will see themselves as cogs rather than as having major roles in the task. Systems that make too many decisions for the user eventually get in the way of the task.
Are able to be modified. Different users have different needs. Systems must be flexible if they are to be able to respond to the needs of the individual.
Are transparent. Systems must be obvious and functionality should be crystal clear. When functionality is hard to find users assume that it is not present and become frustrated by the inability of the tool to support

the task. Systems should be knowledge in the world systems rather knowledge in the head systems.

Support learning. The learner needs extra consideration. Systems should be able to understand the user's position, perhaps even keep a record of the stage the learner has reached. Help should be appropriate and should always be available. Learners should feel as if they are in control but have the support they need.

Support feelings and intuition. People are good at insightful behaviour. People have hunches and gut feelings and systems should support that. Hunches and insightful behaviour are what made human beings into what they are today. A system that prevents intuition is a bad system as it fails to recognize a major element of human characteristics.

Assume that social contact will take place. Human beings are co-operative. Society exists and the people in it interact and co-operate with each other. People like contact with others, this contact helps ideas to develop and leads to feelings of corporate identity. People do not often work in isolation. Indeed, when they do, they are often paid more because it is recognized that being on your own is not something that human beings can in fairness be expected to do as a matter of course. Shneiderman also remarks that lack of contact with other people may have a harmful effect on the emotional well-being of individuals (Shneiderman, 1992).

The development of systems should involve careful consideration of the impact this will have upon the end user. The user has feelings, opinions and intelligence and has a life outside of the organization as well as in it. A system needs to take this into consideration.

7.8 Problems caused by the introduction of computers

Shneiderman (1992) suggests that the introduction and use of computer systems can increase or cause feelings of inadequacy and stress. These considerations need further examination.

Stress and anxiety

Shneiderman argues that quite often systems cause anxiety and stress. It is sometimes difficult for those who are familiar with computers to understand the fear some people have of them. Systems that behave in a seemingly inconsistent and erratic way will increase this anxiety. It has been shown that VDU operators often feel stressed because of things they should not be troubled by, like fear that the printer might not work. It should be the task of system designers to reduce levels of anxiety. Ergonomics takes this on board as a matter of course. If disciplines were not so keen to be divided up, there would not be a problem. Modern students of HCI could do everyone a favour and consider the user in all aspects.

Alienation

Alienation at work is a very common problem. People spend much of their lives working. That experience ought to be pleasurable. For most it is not. Alienated labour is boring labour. It is drudgery. Pheasant (1991) talks about the computerized sweat shops of modern Britain. The thought of workers performing dull, repetitive tasks and glued to VDU screens ought to make society ashamed. Work ought to be fun.

> Someone I know, now retired, told me that when the computer arrived at his work place he stopped knowing what was going on. Before, when he wanted to know the number of repairs performed on a particular product, he worked them out from a list sent in by the repairers. However, the computer took over the task and getting to know what the figures were was difficult. Even worse, the computer seemed unable to give him the piece of information he wanted and in the form he wanted it. All too often, it came in a way that was unnatural or was on a print out that needed a wheel barrow to shift it. That computer was one of the things that drove him to early retirement. The person in charge of the computer became like a huge spider defending a complex web. My friend felt so fly-like in approaching her that he gave up.

Inadequacy

Computers appear to be clever if you do not know how they work. People cannot do the tasks they see computers do that quickly. They think that means that the computer is clever and they are stupid. It should be the aim of HCI experts to overcome these attitudes. The computer is a tool. Those concerned with the development of systems would do well to recite that morning, noon and night. No one feels threatened by pens, televisions, vacuum cleaner or pocket calculators. The computer is an artefact to help users to perform their tasks. Designers should make everything obvious and simple. They should avoid using jargon in front of the novice and should reduce the expertise needed to perform tasks with computers. It does not have to be complicated. If HCI practitioners are experts then the challenge for them is to make it simple for everyone else.

> At South Bank, one of my colleagues tells first year programmers to remember KISS – keep it supremely simple. Those of us in HCI would do well to take that on board.

Systems failures

Systems need to be stable and reliable so that the user does not have to worry about things going wrong or breaking down.

I know of at least one person who followed a PG Dip. course to retrain in computing because the firm she worked for had collapsed under the strain of computerization. Sometimes, it might be necessary to warn organizations that now is not the time to do this.

Lack of privacy

Sometimes employees and customers think that computers seem to know too much. They worry about the safety of the data. One estate agent had its list of computerized sales stolen, along with some keys. My blood runs cold at the thought.

Even worse, some employers think it smart to use the system to spy on their workers. This is a recipe for disaster.

Fear of unemployment

Employees will often wonder if computers cause unemployment. People fear that they might. Socio-technical design has to take this fear on board.

Loss of responsibility

Some employees feel that the computer has taken over their responsibility. They no longer feel necessary or important. They feel that they are there to serve the system.

The classic case of loss of responsibility must be the person in charge of the oven temperature for biscuit baking who was given a computer to help. At first he was delighted, he thought that using a computer would add to his skills. Later, he felt inadequate as his responsibility had gone. Socio-technical design would ensure that the loss of responsibility in one area was compensated for by responsibility given in another area.

Deterioration of self image

Some people are left feeling that their skills are no longer needed or useful.

The graphic artist I mentioned in an earlier chapter felt a sense of loss using the computer rather than pencil and paper. What he was mourning was loss of skill. He was glad to have acquired computing skills. But in a sense that new skill does not compensate for the loss of the old one. The advent of DTP has meant that many people have decided to produce their own publications, posters and the like. He feels that the need for his talents has been stolen by the computers.

Systems must not degrade users. The people working with computerized systems must feel that they are in charge of the system and that the computer is a tool to make their work easier. They must not feel that the computer is in charge of them and they are merely hitting buttons.

7.9 Managing computerization using socio-technical design

Those in management positions need to consider the following when systems are introduced:

1 Strategic planning should consider the effect of the computerization well in advance of its occurrence. It is no good telling workers after the event, the effects upon staff should be considered and staff should be kept informed.

   One workplace I know of introduced a computer system overnight. The staff came in one morning to find it there. That system never operated successfully and finally it became obvious that an alternative would have to be found.

2 Sections of the organization should 'own' parts of the automation. This will put them in control of the systems rather than the other way around. The report of the inquiry into the London Ambulance Service, 1993 cites the lack of this sense of ownership as a contributary factor to the final failure of the system on 4th November 1992 (LAS, 1993).

3 Employees should be involved in the process of automation. If they are involved they will feel responsible and the system is much more likely to work as people do not like to fail. If the system is partly developed by them they will feel responsible for making it a success. This also means that complaints and suggestions about the system can be gathered easily.

4 Jobs might need to be redesigned for all of the reasons discussed above. This should be an opportunity to consider the ergonomics of the workplace.

5 The needs of health and safety have to be considered. Again, this might mean the redesign of particular jobs. The implications of health and safety issues will be examined in a later chapter.

6 Discrimination has to be considered and the legal aspects have to be considered. These aspects will be considered in the final chapter of this book.

7.10 Dialogue design guidelines

A variety of factors are at work in the design and development of the user interface.

In order to produce a suitable design for a human–computer system it is necessary to consider the following:

- the task the user is performing
- the environment in which the system will operate
- the nature of the user

The language of the interface will bear a direct relationship to the nature of the task, its environment and the user type. Thus the language used for the interface of an air-traffic control system will not be the same as that used in the development of an expert system to monitor a heart patient.

Guidelines for the development of interfaces have been developed by a number of experts in the field. Extensive studies have been made by Smith and Mosier (1986), for example. These guidelines are very extensive and obviously there is insufficient space to look at them in detail. Instead the following general principles can be applied when designing systems for people.

7.11 General principles for system design

The basic guidelines can be summarized as follows.

Systems should make sense and be logical. Logicality in design is of paramount importance. This means that tasks should follow on logically and naturally from each other. The user ought to be able to 'expect' what might be required or what might happen next. There should be no surprises, except in game playing systems. The dialogue language and structure should make sense and be predictable.

Systems should be appropriate to the task. The interface and its supporting dialogue should be appropriate to the task being performed. The user and the task domain will impose particular requirements upon the application. The system must support those requirements and the user performing them.

Systems should be consistent. Interface items should be displayed in the same place. The same commands should apply for the same actions. The same keystrokes should be used for the same actions. Do not surprise the user. Do not change things unless there is a good reason for the change and then make it a big one or the user may not notice.

Systems should be forgiving. Systems should be user-friendly and resilient. Human beings can be unpredictable and the system ought to be able to survive that. Users should feel that they are part of a well-designed human–computer system where each part of the system contributes its best. The designer of a system may need to consider the principle of forgiving systems when it comes to the presentation and language of error messages and the nature of the user's tasks at the workstation. Figure 7.1 shows an error message from a GUI system. It warns the user

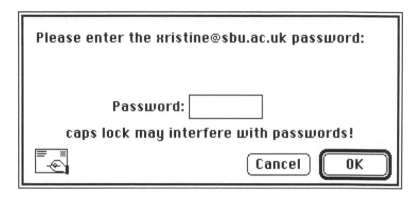

Figure 7.1 *Error message from a GUI (Eudora)*

that the shift key is down and this may affect the password. Figure 7.2 shows what happens when the user types in the wrong username/password to a command line system.

Systems should contain the minimum necessary. Users have mental and physical limitations. The designer of a system needs to consider these when developing the interface and the system. Screen clutter should be avoided; too much noise, too much going on at once makes a system hard to learn. The user will otherwise become overburdened and overburdened users are error prone and erratic because they become stressed.

Systems should be flexible and adaptable. All people are not the same. Their reaction times, their ability to perform without error, their preferences, determination, abilities are all different. A system that can adapt to the person who is using it and the task that the user wants to perform is a good system.

Systems should be fun. Sometimes I think society has forgotten what fun is. There is no reason at all why work or study should not be fun.

**Username: ᴋRISTINE
Password:
User authorization failure**

Figure 7.2 *Error message from a command line system (VMS/VAX)*

A system one of my students developed had a button to take users to the next screen. At the end of the series instead of producing a greyed out button to indicate that it was not possible to go further, there was the usual notice that the user was at the last screen and if the user attempted to click the next button it got up and ran off.

7.12 Summary

Usability engineering strives to ensure that the system will do all the things that the user requires of it and in the best possible way for that particular user.

The object of usability engineering is to ensure that the system meets the criterion of fitness for purpose required by the user.

Usability engineering applies a series of metrics to the systems and then measures the performance of the system against criteria which have been pre-determined by the evaluator and the user.

The additions of Holtzblatt, Bennett and Whiteside will allow for the trading off of various parts of the system and will also enable comparisons to be made between various systems.

The aim of socio-technical design is to fit the process of design into the framework of the needs of the organization. It aims to ensure that the users get the product that fits their task and the particular environment in which they work.

Systems should support users in their tasks. They should be easy to learn, easy to use and easy to understand.

7.13 Self test list

learnability
socio-technical design
throughput
Taylorism
usability
usability enginneering
usability metrics
usability specification

7.14 Exercises

1   Choose a particular group of individuals and make a list of factors you would consider important in designing a system for them.
2   Some organizations are loath to allow their employees to have personalized systems or personal objects in their work areas. Make a list

of the advantages and disadvantages of such an attitude. What do you think?

3 You have been asked to help in the development of a package for maintaining a database that is used for gathering and inputting information about product availability. The workers have never used computers before. They are aged between 25 and 55 and both sexes are represented. The average length of employment is 3 years.

What problems would you expect to encounter with the development of a package for this particular user group? Give reasons for your answer.

4 You are involved in the development of a system for a small kitchen-design firm. The package you have developed is to be used by expert designers who have no previous computer experience. The package will assist in the design process. The interface is to be a GUI. The staff have been there a long time and have no intention of moving on.

What sort of user level would you aim the new system at and why? How would socio-technical design be useful here? What would be your priorities in the development of this system? Give reasons for your answer.

5 Examine the recommendations for system design. How far do you agree with them? Can you add any others?

6 Think of a package you know well. How far does it conform to the design principles discussed in this chapter and elsewhere? Where does it differ?

7.15 References

Bjorn-Andersen, N. (1985) 'Are "human factors" human?' in Bevan, N. and Murray, D. (eds) *Man–Machine Interaction: State of the Art Report*. Maidenhead: Pergamon.

LAS (1993) *Report of the Inquiry into the London Ambulance Service*, London: LAS.

Mumford, E. and Sutton, D. (1991) 'Designing Organisational Harmony and overcoming the failings of current IT methodologies' in *The Computer Bulletin* August, 12–14.

Pheasant, S. (1991) *Ergonomics, Work and Health*, London: Taylor and Francis.

Smith, S. L. and Mosier, J. N. (1986) 'Design Guidelines for Designing User Interface Software'. *Technical Report MTR-10090*, The Mitre Corporation, Bedford, MA 01730, USA.

Shneiderman, B. (1992) *Designing the User Interface*, Reading, MA: Addison–Wesley.

Whiteside, J., Bennett, J. and Holtzblatt, K. (1988) 'Usability Engineering: our experience and evolution' in *Handbook of Human–Computer Interaction*, Amsterdam: North-Holland.

7.16 Further reading

Hix, D. and Hartson, H. (1993) *Developing User Interfaces*, New York: Wiley.
This is is an excellent book on usability and has plenty of exercises.

LAS (1993) *Report of the Inquiry into the London Ambulance Service.* London: LAS.
This is an excellent report for anyone interested in what happens when usability engineering and socio-technical design are ignored. The report is thorough, perceptive and understanding; a must for anyone interested in HCI.

Nielsen, J. (1993) *Usability Engineering*, London: Academic Press.
Is the text that brings all the ideas together. It provides an historical perspective which is interesting.

Jordan, P.W. *et al.* (eds) (1996) *Usability Evaluation in Industry*, London: Taylor and Francis.
After I wrote this chapter I was sent this book. It consists of various chapters written by evaluators. Normally I loathe such collections. They remind me of boxes of chocolates – there are too few of the ones I like and loads I don't like. However, this one is a treat. It is highly readable and refreshingly honest. It is well worth reading for the questions it poses and for its candour.

Norman, D. and Lewis, C. (1987) 'Designing for Error' in Buxton and Baecker (eds) *Readings in HCI*, San Mateo, CA: Morgan Kaufmann.
This paper is one of the best on error. It is funny and challenging and Norman and Lewis probably at their best.

Pheasant, S. (1991) *Ergonomics, Work and Health*, London: Taylor and Francis.
Pheasant's chapter on software ergonomics ought to be compulsory reading for those interested in HCI.

CHAPTER 8
Ergonomics, health and safety

Chapter overview

This chapter examines some of the aspects of ergonomics that are of interest to those who wish to design computerized systems. It looks at some of the health and safety issues which should also be considered.

The main areas of concern to be examined in this chapter are as follows:

- postural fatigue
- repetitive strain injuries
- visual fatigue/disorders
- reproductive disorders
- skin rashes
- stress

8.1 Health and safety

There are a number of health and safety regulations that now apply to the use of VDUs. It is important that both employers and employees ensure that these are understood and applied. The appropriate bodies can provide copies of the current regulations and the Trade Unions and other interested bodies can provide suitable interpretations of the regulations. The principal UK statutory principles are contained in The Health and Safety at Work Act of 1974. This has been modified over the years because of the need to comply with EC directives under Article 118A of the Treaty of Rome. The so-called 'Framework Directive' (89/391/EEC) was adopted in June 1989 and resulted in the 'Six Pack' of UK regulations which include the Health and Safety (Display Screen Equipment) Regulations 1992 and the Provision and Use of Work Equipment Regulations 1992 which also includes VDUs. Enforcement of the regulations is carried out by the Health and Safety Executive. Where regulations overlap it is assumed that the more stringent requirement prevails. The display screen regulations apply to all 'alphanumeric or graphic displays' regardless of the display process involved. These regulations will not be examined in any depth in this book since they are liable to change. The reading list will suggest suitable sources where up to date information can be obtained.

8.2 Postural fatigue and repetitive strain injury

Effort

There are two kinds of muscular effort, **dynamic effort** and **static effort**. An example of static effort might be holding a heavy shopping basket at arm's length. An example of dynamic effort might be turning a wheel. In a computerized environment static effort will be expended keeping the body in an upright position and in maintaining the position of the shoulders and the neck. Dynamic effort will be expended by the muscles of the hand, fingers and wrists.

Static effort consists of a prolonged state of muscle contraction. The muscles are not permitted to relax and it may imply a constrained posture. It is characterized by there being no visible performance. In other words, it is not clear that someone maintaining static effort is actually doing anything.

Dynamic effort consists of a rhythmic alteration between contraction and relaxation of the muscles. In contrast to static effort, when a person is taking part in dynamic effort something is quite clearly being done and the effort is obvious.

During dynamic muscular effort the muscles act as a pump for the blood's circulation. Compression squeezes blood out of the muscles and relaxation causes it to flow in. The muscle may receive 10 or 20 times the amount of blood it receives when it is resting. During dynamic muscular effort the muscle is flushed with blood which supplies it with high energy sugar and oxygen and removes waste products. Dynamic effort can be carried on for long periods of time without fatigue if a suitable rhythm is maintained.

During static muscular effort the blood vessels are compressed by the internal tension of the muscle tissue so that blood no longer flows through the muscle. Waste products are not removed and they accumulate. It is this build up of waste products that causes the acute pain known as muscular fatigue.

If a muscle's effort reaches 60 per cent of its maximum then blood flow is almost completely interrupted. During lesser efforts it restarts. When effort is 15 to 20 per cent of the maximum then blood flow is nearly normal. Static effort which reaches 50 per cent of the maximum can be sustained for not more than one minute. If it is less than 20 per cent then static effort can be sustained for longer. Static work can be sustained for several hours without fatigue provided that effort does not exceed 8 per cent of the maximum.

Examples of static work:

- jobs which involve bending the back forwards or sideways
- holding items with the arms
- lifting the arms horizontally
- standing still for a long time
- bending the head downwards or upwards
- lifting the shoulders for long periods

Even moderate static work can produce fatigue in the muscles involved. This can lead to severe pain. If this is repeated daily over a long period of time then more or less permanent aches will occur. This can lead to damage to joints, tendons, ligaments. This damage can be permanent.

Current advice suggests that 5 to 15 minutes rest pauses are needed for every hour of VDU use. Five minutes would be fine if the conditions are good extending to 15 minutes if conditions are poor, stressful or dull. Possibly, 10 minutes rest is better every hour than 20 minutes after 2 hours.

Repetitive strain injury

Repetitive strain injury (RSI) is an injury caused by a repeated movement and is affecting increasing numbers of VDU operators. Keyboard operators are in one of the highest risk categories. Current theory suggests that using the keyboard at rates above 10,000 keystrokes an hour puts the operator at risk from RSI. The amount of time spent at the keyboard appears to increase the risk of RSI (Horowitz, 1992). It has to be remembered that keying rates for data entry are higher than for other office jobs. A good copy typist is unlikely to exceed 7000 keystrokes an hour, on average, over the working period. However, data entry clerks can reach speeds of 20,000 keystrokes an hour and 12,000 is considered the entry level. The copy typist will have the keystroke load spread fairly equally over both hands but the data entry clerk is likely to use one hand only (Pheasant, 1991).

Another possibility is that RSI may be more likely to develop in those who are suffering from stress. Stress does cause muscular tension and it could be that this is a factor. The studies are as yet inconclusive (Horowitz, 1992; Pheasant, 1996).

Many of the recommendations for the prevention of postural fatigue are also useful for preventing RSI, in other words equipment has to be properly adjusted and regular rest breaks taken. Ideally, jobs should be redesigned so that employees are not expected to spend all day at a VDU. Interestingly, it has been suggested that smokers may be at less risk of developing RSI because they take periodic breaks away from the terminal in order to smoke! (Horowitz, 1992.)

It has to be remembered that RSI is not a modern disease. Tennis elbow and housemaid's knee are both examples of RSI.

Ergonomic keyboards are said to help to reduce the chances of RSI. Some users who have been diagnosed as suffering from RSI and have been advised to discontinue their use of the keyboard, or who have found that using the conventional keyboard is too painful, have found that the ergonomic keyboards enable them to continue to work with keyboards. An example of an ergonomic keyboard is shown in Figure 8.1

However, it must be said that the best treatment for RSI is to avoid it in the first place, by keeping keying in speeds at a reasonable level and taking regular

Figure 8.1 *An ergonomic keyboard*

breaks. Heavy striking of the keys is perhaps the culprit in some cases. Rowe cites 30 journalists at the *Financial Times* (Rowe, 1990) who have been diagnosed as having RSI and have since been offered compensation (Bentham, 1996). It is possible that these people may be amongst those keyboard operators who have not been taught to touch type and tend to use a few fingers on one or both hands rather than all fingers on both hands. If they learned to type on a mechanical typewriter then the temptation will be to strike the keys too hard thus increasing the risks of damage to the hands.

Postural fatigue

A survey conducted by Magora (1972) looked at the incidence of low back pain in over 3000 workers. Magora categorized their work in terms of time spent sitting, standing and lifting. He found that workers who rarely sat, stood or lifted complained of low back pain almost twice as much as those who often sat, stood or lifted. Those who sometimes sat, stood or lifted in the course of their working day rarely experience low back pain. It would seem that doing tasks which require a variety of stances is likely to reduce the likelihood of low back pain.

Eyes fatigue/disorders

The most commonly reported complaints made by VDU operators are of eye strain. This includes loss of visual sharpness, difficulty in focusing, sore eyes, seeing coloured fringes, double vision, grittiness or dryness of the eyes, redness and watering of the eyes. Haider showed that visually demanding work led to visual fatigue but that 75 per cent recovery occurred after 11 minutes and recovery was complete after 16 minutes (Haider, 1980).

VDU work is visually very demanding, it involves tasks for the eye which are different from traditional office work but it is a moot point as to whether the demands made on the visual system are any greater. Office work has always been visually demanding but it might be that the nature of VDU work makes different demands that are more likely to cause problems.

For VDU use the eyes are focused at a fixed distance on a vertical image on a bright screen causing the eye muscles to be almost continuously under tension. The problems caused by continuous muscular effort have already been discussed so it is perhaps not surprising that extensive use of a VDU, perhaps up to 8 hours a day, will cause problems for the user's visual system.

The problems for the user are increased where:

- screens are difficult to read because of poor contrast or insufficient spacing between the characters;
- the level of lighting in the room or at the workstation is too bright or too dull;
- there is glare;
- the user is too close to the screen;
- the user is focusing and refocusing on two different sources of information which are at fixed distances.

Screen flicker can cause headaches and eyestrain. The periphery of vision is most sensitive to flicker so the user of a large monitor might be troubled by flicker at the edge of the screen, particularly if the resolution is not very high. Flicker is also likely to be noticed from a nearby machine so it is important to ensure that there is sufficient distance between VDU operators.

There is no evidence that permanent damage is done to the eye by using a VDU. Pheasant suggests that the long term effects ought to be known by now but so far there is insufficient hard data either way to answer the question conclusively (Pheasant, 1991). However, regular eye checks are advisable and employers should provide them. A good optician will carry out certain additional eye tests if informed that a patient works with VDUs.

Contact lens wearers may find their eyes tend to become dryer when they use a VDU. It is possible that the dryness of the atmosphere around a VDU aggravates this problem but VDU operators may well be blinking less than usual. Many contact lens users find that after a while their eyes adjust to the VDU and the dryness disappears but some people find spectacles a more comfortable alternative.

Cataracts

There have been suggestions that VDU use is causing an increase in the number of cataracts in age groups usually considered too young to develop them. Cataracts are usually associated with a genetic disposition and occur in older age groups. There is still insufficient information to prove a link between cataracts and VDU use.

Photosensitive epilepsy

About 0.5 per cent of the population has epilepsy. Jeavons and Harding (1975) estimated that about 1 in 10,000 are sensitive to flickering lights or certain patterns. The flickering of a VDU screen can trigger an epileptic fit in a susceptible person working at it or within visual range of it. A flicker rate of 25 to 50 Hz cycles per second increases the risk of triggering an epileptic fit. Most standard VDUs in Britain have a refresh rate of 50 Hz. Photosensitive epilepsy is rare and usually first occurs between the ages of 10 and 14 so it is unlikely that the first attack would be triggered by a VDU at work (Oborne, 1995). Anyone sufferering from the problem should seek medical advice.

Work done by Wilkins, and Wilkins, Darby and Binnie suggests that the following precautions can help to minimize the probability of an attack (Oborne, 1995):

1 Reducing the area of the retina stimulated by the screen – using small screens, using light characters on a dark background, limiting the amount of text that appears on the screen and making sure the VDU user sits further back from the screen.
2 Reducing the overall luminance of the screen – the VDU user could wear tinted spectacles, for example.
3 Reducing the screen surround contrast.

Eye infections

Dirty keyboards may account for some eye infections. VDU users' eyes become tired, sore and itchy and they quite understandably rub them. It is easy to imagine how infections might be spread in this way. Keyboards should be kept clean and the area around the VDU kept clear of dust so far as is possible. VDU users should be encouraged to resist rubbing sore eyes. If it is necessary to rub them then the right hand should be reserved for the right eye and the left hand for the left eye. In this way there is less likelihood of spreading infection from one eye to another. Incidentally, if eye drops are used, whether for contact lenses or not, then it is advisable to use two bottles and to keep one specifically for the right eye and one for the left.

I always tell my students to use the back of the hand which is less likely to put dirt from the keyboard into the eyes and may prevent the spread of infection. My own optician recommends closing the eyes tight and rolling the eyeball behind the closed lid. This needs some practice but it may well cut down on the risk of eye complaints.

Reproductive disorders

The research carried out so far is inconclusive, there are many factors and they are difficult to isolate. The major areas of concern are miscarriages and poor pregnancy outcomes, disturbances to the menstrual cycle and low sperm count.

Research carried out on over 2000 women members of the IRSF aged between 16 to 35 was inconclusive though it did find a link between menstrual disorders and stress. It could be that VDU work is more stressful and as this affects the outcome of pregnancy, Grandjean suggests that women workers who are pregnant should not have to work with VDUs if they do not want to since if they are forced to this could have a detrimental effect upon their health (Grandjean, 1987). In the absence of clear-cut evidence either way, this would seem to be a humane and sensible attitude to adopt. Stress has certainly been implicated in disturbances to the menstrual cycle.

One possible explanation for problems experienced by pregnant workers might be that some workstations are poorly designed and workers sit for too long at them. Cramps, aches and pains are not infrequent in pregnancy and the constrained posture workers are forced into by the workstation may well be a factor. It might also be interfering with blood flow. All workers – pregnant or otherwise – should ensure that they have regular breaks away from the workstation. A few minutes break will do much to make a VDU worker feel better and may well reduce the problems that have been cited as possibly caused by VDU work.

The problem with the research so far is that it is not possible to isolate VDU use as the cause of poor pregnancy outcomes. It could be that the women used in the various studies were older and therefore liable to be in a higher risk category as the risk of miscarriage is greater as the woman's age increases. We could simply be looking at the effects of stress. If working with VDUs is harmful in pregnancy then it is more likely to cause a problem in the early stages of pregnancy when the foetus is developing. The problem is that some women may not realise they are pregnant during those early stages. It has to be remembered too that early miscarriages, that is during the first 3 months, are far more frequent than late ones.

It has been suggested that sperm count is affected by VDU use (Bentham 1996). Sperm count appears to be affected by a variety of factors. A recent newspaper report suggested that sperm count was affected by driving. The extra heat given off by VDUs could be a cause as sperm are affected by body temperature. Sperm count also seems to be affected by stress.

Skin rashes

Some VDU operators have complained of skin rashes on the neck, face and chest. These appear after a few hours of VDU work and then disappear over night or when the worker is away from the workstation. Electrostatic discharge from the monitor is a possible culprit.

Some skin rashes have been more persistent. Grandjean, for examples, describes one particular organization that went to considerable effort to cure the skin rashes suffered by its VDU operators (Grandjean 1987). The cause was never satisfactorily identified although stress may well have been a contributory factor.

Stress

It has been suggested VDU work is stressful. Sometimes the stress seems to be caused by shortcomings in the workstation itself and it is hoped that good design of both workstation and environment will prevent this. Another cause of stress appears to be in the design of jobs which involve the use of workstations. If this is the case, then it can be tackled by redesigning the tasks done by the employee to include a variety of activities and rest breaks.

In designing work patterns it would be wise to take account of reaction time, movement time and the problems of attention and to design on the basis that it is pointless expecting the user to be able to react at peak levels at all times since to do so would undoubtedly cause stress. The effect of boredom in creating feelings of stress should not be over looked here, either.

It is important to ensure that the workplace is pleasant and comfortable and that employees have enough space to do their work and to have their personal items around them. This means providing enough storage space for belongings and outdoor clothing and space on the desk or nearby for photographs, plants or whatever else makes them feel comfortable.

8.3 Ergonomics

Ergonomics attempts to make sure that the task is structured to fit the person performing it. It deals with making the performance of task more pleasant and efficient. It enables the design of the working environment and the workplace to conform to the needs of people, their capabilities and how they prefer to perform. In the first instance it is necessary to consider the physical capabilities of the user and the restrictions these will place on the construction of the human–computer system.

Employers are beginning to realize that a good working environment produces happier workers and better work (Hadley, 1996). This means that more thought is being given to office furniture, lighting and decor. A high staff morale means low staff turnover, highly levels of motivation and superior work.

Designing systems for people

It is an interesting exercise to imagine what a user ought to look like by examining the physical requirements of a typical workstation. My students

Figure 8.5 *The upright position*

beneath the window. This is a custom made computer table and is piled high with manuals!

The keyboard

The recommendations made by Pheasant (1991) and generally accepted are:

- A keyboard of 30 mm thickness (measured from the middle row) and tilted 10° to 15° from horizontal.

Figure 8.6 *The laid back position*

- Keys of about 12–15 mm square with a space of 18–20 mm from the centre of one key to another. The keys should be dished and should have a matt surface. Keys that are too small mean that it is easy to hit the wrong key, the same applies if the gap between keys is too small. If keys are too large, users may not be able to reach them. If the gaps between keys are too large then fingers may fall down them! Dished keys are more comfortable for fingers to rest on and prevent slipping.
- Keys should have a resistance of 50–60 g and a travel of 2–4 mm. The should have a positive feel so as to provide the user with a tactile

Figure 8.7 *The footrest*

feedback. Keys that are too sensitive cause extra characters to appear. Keys that offer too much resistance slow the user and mean that more effort has to be made to strike the keys.

Most modern keyboards fulfil all of the above requirements.

There was a craze in the past to set keyboards into a recess in the desk. This helped to cope with the much thicker keyboards that were available then. However, a keyboard set into a recess is fixed and may constrain the user to an unacceptable level. Keyboards should generally speaking be easily moved about the desk so that the user can find the most comfortable position.

Some keyboard operators find wrist rests are useful. Figure 8.10 shows a wrist rest.

Keyboard arrangement

The standard QWERTY keyboard was designed to slow the rate of keying since mechanical keyboards were incapable of keeping pace with fast typists and the keys jammed.

The Dvorak keyboard (designed in 1943) is an alternative design and superior to the QWERTY in terms of performance levels. Some claim 10–20 per cent with less hand and finger fatigue. Norman (1990) suggests the improvement is closer to 10 per cent and says that changing to the Dvorak

Figure 8.8 *A chair for VDU use*

keyboard does not make good sense because of the relearning involved and the cost of replacing keyboards. The relearning is a considerable problem since this would cause the user to suffer from all of the problems of negative transfer examined in an earlier chapter of this book.

Figures 8.11 and 8.12 show the Qwerty and Dvorak keyboards.

Keyboard feel

This is the sense of key travel and resistance and auditory feedback and **hysteresis**. Hysteresis is the tendency for the key switch to remain in a closed

Figure 8.9 *The user tries to fix the problem*

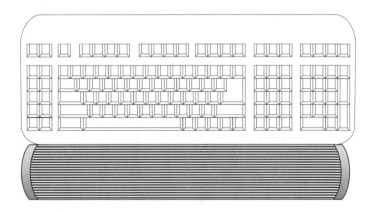

Figure 8.10 *A wrist rest*

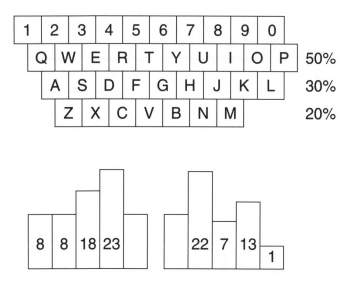

Figure 8.11 *The Qwerty keyboard showing finger strokes of each hand*

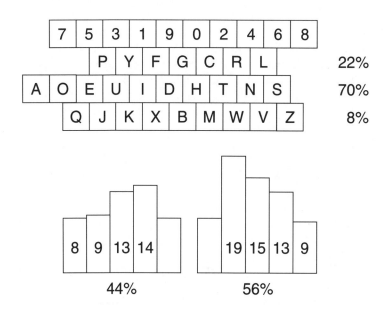

Figure 8.12 The Dvorak keyboard showing finger strokes of each hand

position even after a partial release of downward pressure. It is the difference in travel distance between the opening and closing points of the switch. Too little hysteresis results in keyboard bounce and causes extra characters to be inserted, too little hysteresis slows down the typist and requires more effort.

The screen

The legibility of text is dictated by the size, shape and layout of the characters and by the quality of the visual image. This will determine how easy it is to read the screen from different distances. The closer the reader has to be to the screen the more constrained the body posture and the more quickly the user will suffer from body fatigue and visual tiredness. The image should be free from flicker and any other visually disturbing effects. The colour of the characters appears to be a matter of taste and research in the area has so far been inconclusive and sometimes contradictory. Generally speaking, though extremes of the spectrum are probably best avoided. A viewing distance of at least 500 mm is needed and 750 mm is probably better. A minimum of 3 mm high characters is probably needed; Pheasant says that 4 mm is probably better (Pheasant, 1991). If the reading conditions are not good, people will move closer to the screen.

Characters that are easier to read on the screen are not necessarily easier to read on paper. It is essential to realize that the two experiences are quite different. In one study in 1984 it was shown that people proof-read about 20–30 per cent slower on the VDU than with hardcopy. These results were confirmed in 1987 and 1989. The major problem appears to be image quality so the higher the resolution the less the difference ought to be. Generally speaking, those fonts named after cities: Geneva, Chicago etc. are best used on the screen. Figure 8.13 shows examples of the 'city' fonts. ANSI recommends a minimum height of 2.3 mm (0.09 in.) and a preferred height of 0.116–0128 in. (2.9–3.3 mm) for capital letters at a viewing distance of 20 inches.

There is no general agreement on the best colours for reading text. Some people favour black on white since people are used to reading books like that. However, it is advisable to use as few colours as possible since too many are distracting. This is often described as the Las Vegas effect. It is also advisable to avoid the use of the extremes of the colour spectrum (red and blue). This view is contradicted by some sources (e.g. Matthews *et al.*, 1989).

Chicago

Geneva

Helvetica

New York

Monaco

Figure 8.13 *The 'City' fonts*

8.4 The office environment

The above sections considered the work desk and the seating of the worker. However, there are other considerations to take into account in the design of the computerized office. The following sections will examine the workplace.

Lighting

The more detail the user needs to see, the more light needed to perform the task. The extent to which the performance of a task will be affected by lighting will depend on the visual demands of the task. Satisfaction with lighting increases with the level of illumination and flattens out between 500 and 1000 lux. Grandjean notes that people become dissatisfied with lighting of more than 1000 lux as it creates glare and shadows. An illumination range of 500–700 lux is suitable for general office purposes. An office with lighting of 1000 lux or more is probably over lit unless the work being done is particularly intricate. Desirable levels for VDU use are actually lower and range from 300 to 500 lux. (Grandjean, 1987).

Most people prefer natural daylight and they also like to look outside. People who work in rooms without windows frequently complain of feeling isolated, claustrophobic or depressed. However, glazing can cause problems with heat gain in summer and heat loss in winter.

Glare is the unpleasant visual sensation which occurs when excessively bright objects intrude into the visual field. It causes discomfort to the eyes and headaches, and in extreme cases it can cause damage to the eye.

Recommendations
- There should be no reflection of light either artificial or natural from the screen.
- General room lighting should be between 300 and 500 lux. Lighting should be even and should not create deep shadows.
- Ceiling mounted fluorescent lights should be fitted with diffusers or shields. The VDU user should sit between them. The lights should run parallel to the window and parallel to the user's line of vision.
- Ceiling mounted spot lights should be avoided as they concentrate heat on the user's neck.
- Indirect light is perhaps best.
- Fluorescent lights oscillate at 100 Hz in the UK (120 Hz in the USA). The 100 Hz oscillation is sometimes called 'invisible flicker' because although it might not be consciously perceptible to the user the brain subconsciously registers it. This can cause eye strain and stress. There are new high frequency tubes which are expensive to install but cost less to run. They appear to produce a better light for VDU work.

- There should be task lights where necessary and these should be equipped with a dimmer switch. Task lights enable a user to have more control over the working environment and will increase contentment and reduce stress.
- Windows should be fitted with blinds that are easy to use.
- If a VDU is near a window it should be at right angles to the window. VDU users should not face a window because of exposure to direct glare.
- A VDU screen should not face a window because that would create problems with shadow, reflections and glare.
- There should be temperature control. Rooms housing VDUs can get very hot.

Noise

A noise is a noise when it annoys! Like beauty, noise appears to be subjective. Some people can tolerate higher levels of noise than others, although what activity is being done and how much concentration it requires probably affects what levels of noise can be tolerated.

Exposure to noise can cause permanent damage to the ears. It can also cause stress related responses, lead to loss of balance, affect the heart rate or rhythm, increase blood pressure and affect the general well being of the individual concerned.

It is important that the designers of offices do not expose employees to unacceptable levels of noise. Noise can bother people more than they are aware and can increase stress and interfere with their concentration.

The EC rules permit 40 dB for intellectual work, 60 dB in general offices or 70 dB where telephones are used. Printers should be shielded with a noise-reducing cover where they are liable to be noisy. If possible they should be placed away from the workstation. This will cut down on the noise in the working area and also have the advantage that the user will need to move from the workstation in order to collect printout. This can provide much needed exercise and a break from the workstation. Obviously, if printout has to be gathered frequently the constant walking up and down would be unacceptable.

In Britain the Health and Safety Executive recommends that workers should not be subjected to more than 90 dB for more than 8 hours in any one day. This would be like working near an underground train all day.

8.5 Summary

Good posture and well designed working conditions will probably alleviate most of the difficulties and problems associated with VDU use. A user who is happy and comfortable is more like to work better, make fewer mistakes and less likely to take time off work.

There are two types of muscular effort – dynamic which can be maintained if the right rhythm is obtained, and static which can cause muscular fatigue.

RSI is best prevented rather than cured. Good working practices will do much to alleviate the risks.

Poor screen quality and poor screen design will increase the problems of eye strain. VDU users should try to take regular rest breaks and use the time to stretch muscles and give eyes a rest from the fixed focus position.

It may be that many of the other problems that are raised as possible health issues for VDU users are caused by a stressful environment. Workers who are stressed are likely to succumb to aches and pains. Good working practices and well designed environments will help reduce these problems.

When designing systems, it is important to work within the bounds of the user's capabilities.

Ergonomics attempts to ensure that the task is suitable for the person doing it. A well-designed work area with good equipment that is reliable and pleasant to use will make the user feel valued. Output will be improved.

8.6 Self test list

anthropometry
dynamic effort
hysteresis
laid back position
repetitive strain injury
static effort
upright position

8.7 Exercises

1 Check the viewing distances of some VDU users. What details would you need to record if this was a proper study?
2 What problems are there when we attempt to find out if VDUs can really damage your health?
3 What guidelines could you issue for VDU users?
4 If you know other people who use computers either at home or at work or for study, do a short survey. Find out how much time they spend using a VDU. Do they take rest breaks? What comments do they make about how they feel (physically, mentally) after working with computers? How do you feel? How does this compare with others?

CHAPTER 9

Social implications and the future of HCI

Chapter overview

This final chapter examines the implications of computerization. Obviously, there is insufficient space here to consider all aspects of what it might mean for society so this chapter will only take a brief look at some of the areas that computers have touched on in modern life. In particular, it will examine implications for the workplace, the home, effects on social discourse and legal aspects.

9.1 The workplace

Computers can now be found in all areas of working life. They started out as specialized equipment, used by experts and maintained by many technicians. Nowadays, they can been seen on the desks of the word processor who has replaced the typist to the doctor who might use the system to enter in prescriptions and print them out. Tills have become computerized. What customers can ask of a shop assistant selling books, for example, will be limited by how powerful the particular access system employed by the book shop is. Calculations that once would have been laboriously done manually or with the aid of a calculator can now be done in no time at all on the ubiquitous spreadsheet.

Initially, the introduction of computers into the workplace was not accomplished without problems. There were job changes, retraining and job losses though the latter were not as widespread as was sometimes expected or feared. Most computers introduced into a workplace did not replace employees, but they did change the tasks those employees were doing and undoubtedly some jobs disappeared through natural wastage. The situation may well be changing now. The biggest problems were faced by the employees who had to manage with these new systems. Frequently systems were bought by managers without consultation with the employees who would be using the systems. Managers were often beguiled by demonstrations of clever computer games and animations. There was little done by way of consultation with the employees themselves and finally when the systems were introduced it was frequently shown that there was a mismatch between what the employee needed of the system and what the system was able to provide. For example Brian Bramer of De Montfort University has commented on the number of systems he saw abandoned because typists given them could not make them produce work at the speed and quality they required. Had the typists been asked to try out keyboards, for example, they could have contributed valuable evaluation material prior to the purchase (Bramer, 1988).

A system imposed upon a employee will not be received with the good will and co-operation that the introduction of a new system may require. A system that is imposed can never be greeted with the same optimism and desire to make it work that a system that has been negotiated will automatically bring to its introduction, even if there is no difference between the two systems!

Jobs have been changed by computerization. Many workers have been retrained to use computers. Some are pleased with the new skills they have learned. Others mourn the loss of responsibility or old skills. Some jobs have disappeared or changed beyond recognition. Quite often jobs that would have been done by a secretary, clerk or typist have disappeared because the professionals for whom they would have worked now carry out the task themselves. For example, many lecturers now wordprocess their own examination papers and use quite complex formats for them. A businessman once told me that he thought it might be faster for him to wordprocess much of the highly technical documentation he has to produce because that way he knew it was accurate. The typist would simply format it for him. Perhaps computerization has given more tasks to those who do not need them at the expense of those who needed the work to ensure employment.

For many employees though, computerization has been exciting and rewarding despite the drawbacks. Both the Labour Research Department (LRD) and the Trade Union Congress (TUC) reported in their booklets on the health and safety aspects of VDUs that despite all of the problems, employees were often enthusiastic about the technology, although one employee remarked wryly that perhaps he would not feel the same way in 6 month's time.

Computerization has been seen by many employees as a means of gaining extra skills and finding new interest in their jobs. The rate at which improvements in the systems has occurred has meant that tasks that were previously laborious and time consuming can now be done quickly and efficiently. An examination of early texts on Dbase II, for example will show how far performance has improved.

'We are happy that our computers can trim down to minutes what might take a human hours to perform. But not all of us realize these minutes can be trimmed down to mere seconds.

'Therefore, on a database with 5000 records on it, displaying all the Millers [10] could take as long as 740 seconds (a little over 12 minutes), with a LIST FOR approach. Using an indexed file with the FIND and

LIST WHILE approach will perform the same task in about 45
seconds . . .' (Simpson, 1985)

Today, a search of 5000 records that took as long as 45 seconds would be
slow but it is easy to forget that the original time scale of 12 minutes showed
a vast improvement on what would have been possible manually. Indeed, many
of the tasks that can now be done with a computerized system would not have
been attempted formerly because the cost would have been prohibitive.

But this ability to make tasks easy and quick has meant that some tasks get
done because they can be done and sometimes it is unclear just how useful such
an activity really is. **Information overload**, where individuals are given too
much information to cope with, is unfortunately all too common today.
Employees with much too much to read are often sent on speed reading courses
so that they can get through the vast quantity of written material that they need
to look at. E-mail systems suffer from the automatic delete syndrome whereby
a receiver of e-mail may delete a message without reading it because the sender
is not deemed to have anything important to say or because the subject of the
message may not appear to be relevant.

When a computer is employed for a task, careful consideration needs to be
taken about whether or not the task is really necessary and will achieve
something useful in the end. Simply doing something because it can be done is
not sufficient. Systems can also have too much functionality, display too many
options, ask for too much information. It is very important that a system exists
within the bounds of real need and it does not expect extraordinary behaviour
from the user. Some of the accidents which have been attributed to human error
can be seen as a response to information overload.

The technology has brought some problems, however. Some organizations
were driven into collapse or near collapse because of the strains of
computerization. Others improved their efficiency enormously. For those who
understand the technology the risks of a non-paper based medium are well
understood and the appropriate care can be taken. However, not all organizations realize that disks are not infallible, or that computers can be stolen. Never
a month goes by without my hearing of at least one organization that has lost
important material either because of disks becoming corrupt, equipment being
stolen or backup or security procedures not being followed. It is important that
when systems are sold to businesses and home users that the backup facilities
are discussed at the same time. Many businesses seem to learn the hard way
and even after a disaster they do not always heed the lesson. I know of at least
one organization that has lost material twice!

It is easy to be lulled into a false sense of security over the permanence and
safety of electronic material. Students on computer courses ought to know
better than to trust important work to one floppy disk, or a hard disk but
disasters seem to happen with monotonous regularity. Whilst negotiating a
humane and compassionate settlement for one such student I was surprised to

be told that the course director had no option but to be sympathetic since he had lost the entire contents of a hard disk the month before and his back-ups were less than satisfactory! With such lax attitudes apparent amongst the computer literate it is hardly surprising that people with less experience are unaware of the problems and dangers.

As the nature of the systems becomes more obvious, hopefully some of these problems will disappear. Those trained on manual or electric typewriters are accustomed to producing hard copy as they type. It is difficult for such a user with such a model of a system to understand that until the file is saved or printed out, it does not exist in the same sense.

> One user told me that he had keyed in a lot of work and when he went to save was greeted with 'disk full'. He got scared and switched the computer off. He wondered if I could find his file for him and was dismayed to hear that I could not. It is difficult for novice users to understand that although the material may be on the screen until it is saved it is not possible to think about it as something stable.

9.2 The home

Computers came into the home mostly as game machines and were largely judged on what they could offer. It is amazing to think now of the size of some of those early computers and what could be done with them. The 16K of memory many of us were quite pleased with then would represent a letter today.

These early systems were unstable and temperamental. Many early users would spend all evening trying to load a game from a cassette tape only to have the thing hang up. Today our systems are much more reliable and easy to use.

There have been doubts expressed about the wisdom of allowing children to use computers unsupervised. There are stories of epileptic fits caused by VDUs and video games and some of the material in these games is dubious in content. It is argued that they encourage violence, break down social interaction thus causing social misfits and have also been cited in divorce cases. I was amused to read that as long ago as 1985 Vitalari *et al.* were anxious about the computer user who spent more time on the computer and working alone so that family television viewing time was reduced (cited by Shneiderman, 1992). No doubt when television was first introduced there were worries about how that might intrude upon family life too.

Presumably computers will become more widespread in the home. Already the television adverts suggest that somehow one is lacking in a fundamental if one does not possess a computer nor have access to the internet. But the problem is surely one of degree and how computers are used and that must be the decision of the individual user. The developer of VisiCalc (Apple II) when asked if he used a spreadsheet to organize his home finances replied that if his lifestyle was sufficiently complex to require a spreadsheet, he would change his lifestyle.

9.3 Society

E-mail is altering the way in which communication takes place. It has been around for some time but it is only in the last few years that it has really taken off and this must largely be attributed to the Web and the success stories there. Previously, e-mail was something used by academia and a small number of other organizations. Nowadays one is frequently given an e-mail address on business cards, advertisers quite often cite e-mail addresses or Web sites or perhaps both and private individuals are more likely to say they have e-mail accounts. There are even advertisements which use jokes about e-mail and the WWW. This surely implies a body of potential customers who understand and appreciate the references, though how the public is coping with the e-mail addresses is less clear.

I was much amused by an announcer who gave his e-mail address over the air without spelling his surname which could be spelt in several different ways. Nor did he explain whether the first and second name were joined and if so how. I assume that anyone e-mailing would use trial and error.

It takes less time to type an e-mail message than typing a letter because the format is not so formal. One liners or even one word replies are not uncommon though it is best to refer to small amounts of what was sent as if there is a delay in replying to the e-mail, the recipient may have forgotten what the subject is. Figure 9.1 shows the interface to a command line e-mailing system. Figure 9.2 shows a typical e-mail message on a GUI. The chevrons indicate that the original message is being quoted by the sender. Modern e-mail systems provide this as an automatic facility.

The attitudes to e-mail systems are interesting. A culture has grown up around how it operates and what it can be used for.

One novice user told me he wanted to make his e-mail message look nice. He was effectively typing a letter and began with 'Dear Steve' and ended 'Yours sincerely'. He could not understand how e-mail messages tended not to be like that. At the other end of the scale, one of my close friends complained that his e-mail system had an inbuilt spell checker. He thought that spell checking was not in the spirit of e-mail.

E-mail is not obtrusive like the phone but it gets a reply almost as quickly if the receiver is on-line frequently. It is not necessary to phone back if the person

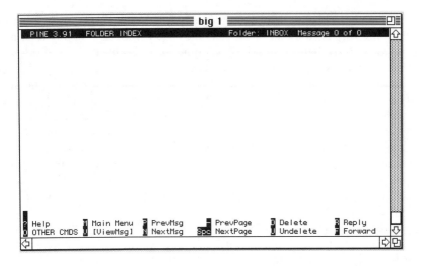

Figure 9.1 *The interface to an e-mailing system (Pine running under unix)*

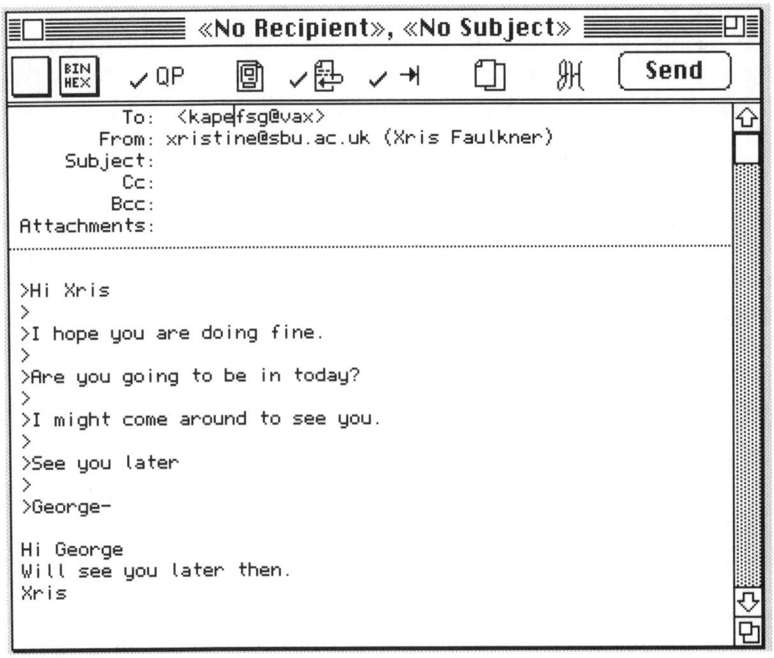

Figure 9.2 *An e-mail message*

you wish to contact is not there and there is no need to worry about whether or not they are busy or in a bad mood. The message can be sent at any time and will be replied to when the receiver has time to deal with it.

However, it does appear to be addictive. One parent writing to an agony aunt was concerned that her son had fallen in love with his net friend. She was worried about the amounts of time he spent e-mailing someone half way across the world and whom he had never met. There have already been net marriages (Urquhart, 1996) and e-mail systems have been cited in divorce cases with one husband claiming his wife was effectively unfaithful because she had a 'virtual' affair (*Evening Standard*, 1996). Interestingly enough while the wife described it as a romantic daydream a survey by the on-line magazine Mr Showbiz showed 29.1 per cent of people thought 'virtual' affairs amounted to adultery.

The attitudes to those who have not had experience with e-mail messages is interesting. Some people find them difficult to envisage. The system is really a cross between a mail system and a telephone in that it is perhaps rather more easy to get the wrong address with an e-mail system than it is via the postal system (now often called 'snail mail' because it takes so long) but the chances are probably not high. Anyone who has made friends via an e-mail system knows how intriguing those relationships can be.

The trouble with current e-mail systems is that what the sender sends is not always what is received the other end. For example, I was warned a long time ago about using £ in e-mail systems after a friend had some difficulty trying to figure out what I might be saying. One never knows quite how they will be interpreted so it is better to write 'pounds' or UKP (United Kingdom Pounds) or GBP.

> One solicitor e-mailing a client to tell him of the size of the deposit required for a business he was purchasing was surprised and pleased to receive a reply that told the seller that the purchaser had no intention of paying such a large deposit. The solicitor had sent a message saying '£5000 deposit' but this has been reinterpreted by the various systems as 'a 35000 deposit'. The purchaser was horrified by the size of the deposit and happened to take the strong stand that the lawyer wished him to make. A happy ending this time, but others might not be quite so lucky.

The systems are not without their problems though. The ease with which text can be cut and pasted into an e-mail communication and the fact that many systems can automatically cite the text being replied to means that many e-mail communications are very lengthy and time consuming to read. The same problem is evident in the newsgroups. At the other end of the scale, some users are prone to send one word or short sentence replies. If there has been a time lag in their sending the reply or if the person being communicated with gets a lot of electronic mail then the drift of the 'conversation' can be lost. At the time of writing one newsgroup interested in law is arguing whether or not e-mail can be said to be a legitimate form of communication and therefore legally binding.

With the growth of artificial intelligence (AI) the expert system grew up very rapidly and has led to the existence of all kinds of systems. There are systems to help monitor diabetes, they are 'virtual' dogs and cats. There are simulations of horses to allow jockeys to learn how to ride without fear of damaging a valuable horse. The Surrey Police use a video computer system to help the police learn how to tackle people with weapons (Hatley, 1996). At the time of writing, there was news of a system developed to help those who wanted euthanasia deliver their own lethal doses (Shears, 1996). Technology can take over all sorts of aspects of our lives and we may have to ask whether some of those tasks are more appropriately handled by a human being. Computers are now used to perform tasks that perhaps would not have been predicted. In the early stages of computerization some writers said that systems were unlikely to be adopted by some of the professions and the medical and legal professions were cited in particular. Many patients though are accustomed to seeing a PC on the desk of the doctor.

> When my own doctor's surgery installed its first computer system I was disappointed to discover that the doctor was not consulting an expert system but merely printing out the prescription. Undoubtedly, it is convenient to have all the data stored on a computer system but I have to sympathize with my own doctor who peering at me, round his VDU said that it ought not be on his desk, it was ugly and big and it got in the way. He added rather poignantly that his was a caring profession and yet the system encouraged him to look at the VDU screen and not at the patient.

Society maybe needs to ask itself whether some of these applications are appropriate. If they are and if these 'caring' tasks are to be carried out by computers then the quality of the software and particularly the aptness of the interface becomes perhaps a matter of life or death. There is no room for mistakes in such systems.

9.4 Hypertext and the Web

A thorough discussion of hypermedia and the World Wide Web (WWW) is too extensive for a book devoted to human–computer interaction, but the problems experienced in the development of such systems are interesting ones from the point of view of human–computer interaction. So it would be useful to examine these systems particularly as they are dominating computing so much with the advent of very powerful multimedia systems and the success of the Web.

A hypertext system consists of a series of pages and links that connect these pages. The links can join any page to any other page and pages may have a

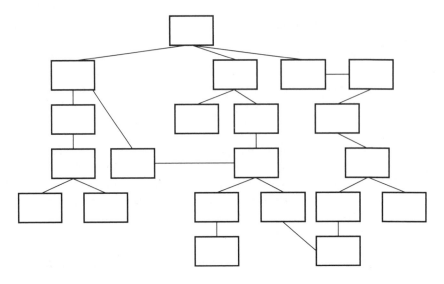

Figure 9.3 *Possible structure of a hypertext system*

number of links in them. Hypertext systems do not have to be linear and the various users of the system do not have to progress through it in the same way. Figure 9.3 shows a possible structure for a hypertext system.

Hypertext systems are designed to be flexible so that the reader is able to use the system in the most appropriate way, according to individual taste, predilections and needs. Hypertext systems may contain pictures, text, sound, animation and so on. The links may be presented as obvious buttons for the user to click on with a mouse, or they may be hidden buttons, or areas of text known as **hot-spots**. These hot-spots are often displayed as bold text and will take the user to a different part of the system. Figure 9.4 shows some common hypertext buttons. Figure 9.5 shows some hot-spots in the form of text. Figure 9.6 is a typical Web interface.

The biggest problem with hypertext systems is that users get lost and do not always know where they are or where they are going. Users who feel lost in hyper space exhibit all of the responses that we would expect to see in someone who is physically lost. Builders of hypertext systems have endeavoured to overcome the problems of navigation by providing a map of where the user has been or even a map of the whole system. Figure 9.7 shows a map produced for a hypertext system on the Greek Gods. Some systems place 'foot prints' on the page that a user has visited, or produce 'back' buttons that can take the user back through the system, in the reverse order. Even so users still often complain that they do not know where they are in relation to things they have seen and worse they are unsure where they need to go next. My students, developing hypermedia systems have used the usual tricks for ensuring the user feels in control but nevertheless we continue to experience problems with 'lost' users.

There have been some interesting interface problems posed by such systems. Figure 9.8 shows the interface to a system built recently. This system provides a guide to the Minoan Temple at Crete. The user of the system is able to navigate around the temple, look at the various parts of the building, the museum, the artefacts and read about the temple. It is possible to visit the temple in any order and to zoom in on points of interest. The system uses sound and video and is vastly entertaining and interesting. However, during user trials the student who built it noticed some very strange and interesting responses. Some users became confused by buttons labelled 'previous' which took them to a page they had previously visited and 'back' which took them to the page before the one they were on, but not necessarily one they had seen. Buttons

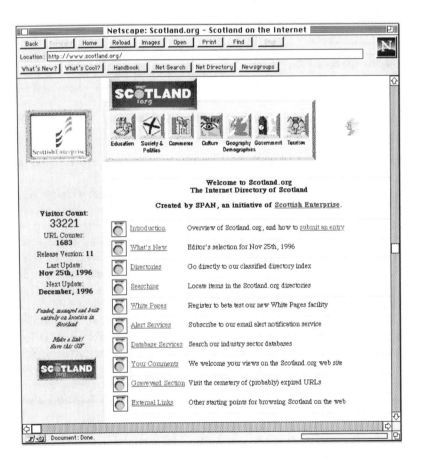

Figure 9.4 *A hypertext document showing buttons*

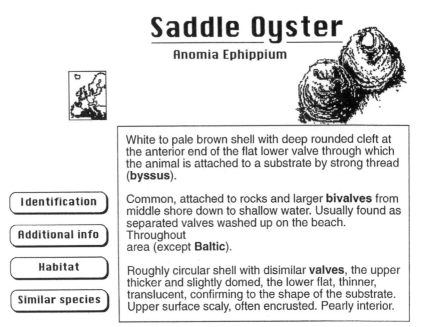

Saddle Oyster

Anomia Ephippium

Identification

Additional info

Habitat

Similar species

White to pale brown shell with deep rounded cleft at the anterior end of the flat lower valve through which the animal is attached to a substrate by strong thread (**byssus**).

Common, attached to rocks and larger **bivalves** from middle shore down to shallow water. Usually found as separated valves washed up on the beach. Throughout area (except **Baltic**).

Roughly circular shell with disimilar **valves**, the upper thicker and slightly domed, the lower flat, thinner, translucent, confirming to the shape of the substrate. Upper surface scaly, often encrusted. Pearly interior.

Figure 9.5 *A hypertext document showing the presence of hot-spots*

labelled 'previous' and 'back' are common occurrences in hypermedia systems.

Apart from lost users the other two most pressing problems with the Web are latency and content. The problem of latency refers to the long waits users have to endure whilst waiting for pages to load. This is an interesting problem because, of course, many of us who have used computers for some time can remember how slow the systems used to be. In the early days, those teaching HCI would suggest that users would be tolerant of a 1 second delay but delays of over 5 seconds needed some indication as to what was going on. Longer delays needed the user to be alerted prior to the action that would cause the delay. As the power and speed of the systems increased so the problem of having to wait disappeared. It seems we are back with the problem of delay and how to cope with it. Obviously, the best solution is to fix the problem but until that occurs it is necessary to give users indications of how long things will take and that something is happening. Otherwise they click mice, issue commands and cancel actions in the misguided impression that something has gone wrong. Unfortunately, that is sometimes the case.

Working on this book today and waiting for pages to be printed I was reminded of how printing or screen savers and so on can cause information to be lost from the screen. Often all that remains of a system message is the box! This evening, faced with the two usual print boxes without words in and a third larger one in the centre of the screen, again without words in it, I was forced to conclude that the system had hung up and was probably suggesting I reboot. But I have to admit my conclusion was largely based on guesswork. A novice faced with a situation like that may well panic.

If clocks are shown on the screen to show that time is passing and something is happening then they ought to be animated. The hands of clocks move unless they have stopped. A clock or watch that does not appear to be moving may well worry a user. Likewise bars showing the percentage of task carried out so far need to move and show a real relationship to what is happening. The Web

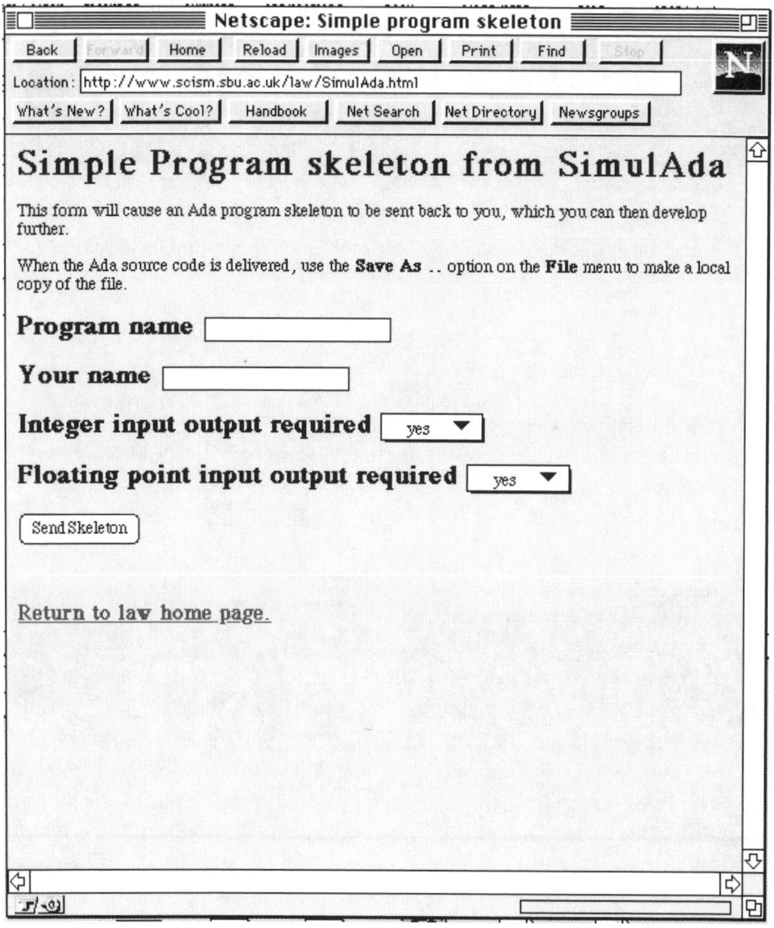

Figure 9.6 *A WWW interface*

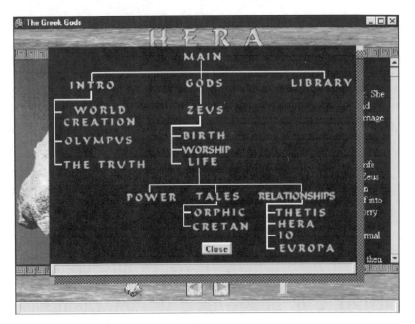

Figure 9.7 *A map of a hypertext system – The Greek Gods (built with ToolBook)*

Figure 9.8 *MINOAS*

shows transfer rate and percentage transfer carried out so far. Some of the figures displayed are clearly fanciful. They do need to relate to what the user is experiencing.

The problem of content will become more serious as time passes unless something is done to help users find what they want and ignore the rubbish. There is a wealth of information of the Web. Some of it is useful and well presented. Some is useless and badly presented. All areas in between are clearly represented. Some people are calling for checks and restrictions. The same argument was offered recently about the internet and the newsgroups, that they needed to be controlled and regulated. If users had a clearer idea where they were in relation to the information they sought and could easily store information about where they might want to go again then the problem is reduced. Although the bookmarks are in theory a good idea, they require the user to remember what it was that was useful about the location. Furthermore, the user does have to make a conscious effort to store the location as a bookmark. The problem of content is probably related to a lack of under-standing about what can usefully be displayed on screen and how it is best displayed. That problem is one addressed by HCI. Until Web page developers address the problems of making pages easy to navigate and interesting to interact with on-line it is difficult to see how the problem can be resolved. It would be sad if the Web disappeared under a volume of rubbish but at the same time too stringent a control might well spoil what should be an exciting medium.

9.5 Computer systems and the law

Health and Safety at Work

Health and safety issues in the United Kingdom have been dealt with in the previous chapter, however it is worth commenting that health and safety issues surrounding the design of an interface will depend to some extent on the market for the system and its intended use. For example, a product which is to be used by the military may have different health and safety requirements from those of commerce. Likewise, health and safety issues vary from country to country.

Health and safety legislation is a rapidly developing area of law, particularly within the European Community, and it is important that developers take advice from suitable professionals on the health and safety aspects of the product at the development stage. This is particularly important where a foreign market is concerned as the developers may not be aware of the requirements. Though the law looks backwards for case precedents, software developers are at the forefront of a developing technology and must do their best to anticipate trends within the expected life of the product.

Copyright law and software

Issues of copyright can range from the simple plagiarising of code, the unlicensed use of modules or development tools to questions of the 'look and feel' of a system.

Within the EC software is specifically subject to the laws of copyright. In the UK, programs and sound recordings are covered under The Copyright, Designs and Patents Act 1988 which also makes it a 'restricted act' to store a work in a computer. Interestingly, the Patents Act 1977 S1(2) and Article 52 of the European Patent Convention explicitly bars computer programs from being patented. The 1988 Act permits decompiling of programs if it is necessary to obtain information not readily obtainable elsewhere and provided it is carried out by or on behalf of a licensed user for the purpose of creating an independent, inter-operable but non-competing program.

At the time of writing, databases give rise to copyright problems in that the contents if 'mere sweat of brow' are not subject to copyright but the means of storage, compression retrieval etc. might be so covered. This is an area which is likely to see rapid legal developments over the next few years as interested parties attempt to profit from the packaging of public information.

Copying software is an infringement of copyright and it is a criminal offence for someone to breach that copyright, also the copyright owner has the right to recover damages under the terms of the 1988 Act which include any benefit accruing to the defendant. In addition, the offending goods may be seized by the holder of the infringed copyright even if they have been passed on to a third party.

Look and feel is more subtle problem and there will presumably be more legal skirmishes.

Liability for defective software

Liability is an area which should any software developer needs to consider, from the pre-contract stage through to final delivery of the product and thereafter during maintenance. The actual contractual terms are a problem for lawyers but the developer can help by ensuring that a proper and detailed specification is drawn up in discussion with the client and is formally agreed. The usability engineering approach should guarantee that this does indeed occur and should enable an assessment of fitness for purpose to be made.

It is vital that the specification and in particular any variations are properly documented. Many of the problems that have arisen because of allegedly defective software can be linked to poor product specification and unrealistic expectations on the part of the user. The problems with the software designed for the London Ambulance is a good example of lack of careful specification and perhaps a lack of understanding between developer and customer (LAS, 1993). It is important to note here that 'unrealistic expectations' is a somewhat relative term and what is unrealistic today may be entirely reasonable in the near future.

Many so called defective products are simply products which do not meet the client's expectation. That is not to say that such clients may not have valid cause for complaint because a product that does not meet user expectations may well be defective. An interface which is awkward or difficult to use may render the product defective to the extent that the client is entitled to reject it. For example, under the Sale of Goods Act it could be argued that the software was not of satisfactory quality. On the other hand, it could be that the use of unsatisfactory or defective software or negligence on the part of the provider results in loss or damage to the client thereby creating a potential liability.

9.6 Summary

Computers can now be found in all areas of working life. Their introduction caused some problems and led to job changes and retraining. Inappropriate systems were sometimes introduced by managers who knew little about the needs of the employers and who failed to consult their workforce.

For many employees computerization has been exciting and rewarding. It has led to extra skills and has often created more interesting work.

It is easy to use a computer to do tasks that do not really need to be done and care should be taken to ensure that time is not wasted doing something just because it can be done.

Not all organizations are careful about their information. Electronic copy needs to be treated with the same respect and care as hard copy and back ups are needed.

Computers came into the home mostly as game machines. Their role is still evolving and developing.

E-mail is a new and efficient means of communication but there are important security matters to be considered.

Society maybe needs to ask itself whether some of the applications computers are used for are appropriate.

A system is a flexible series of pages and links that connect these pages. They do not have to be linear and users can progress through them in any way they choose. Helping users to navigate through such systems is not easy.

Health and Safety legislation is a rapidly developing area of law and it is important that developers take advice from suitable professionals at an early stage.

Issues of copyright range from the plagiarising of code to questions of the 'look and feel' of a system.

Liability for defective software is an area which any software developer needs to consider. The usability engineering approach should guarantee that systems are fit for use.

9.7 Self test list

hot-spot
information overload

9.8 Exercises

1 Examine some different computer systems or applications. Try to identify what you like and dislike about them. Where are they similar and where are they different?

2 If you have access to e-mail you might like to make a record of your e-mail, snail mail, telephone calls etc. for a week. Examine the data. What does it tell you about your methods of communication? Do you prefer one method over another and if so why?

3 Examine some WWW sites. Which are the most interesting and why? Do you experience any feelings of being lost and if so why and when do they occur?

9.9 References

Bramer, B. (1988) 'Problems of software portability with particular reference to engineering CAE/CAD systems.' *Computer Aided Engineering Journal*, September 233–236.

'Cybersex was only a dream says wife,' *The Evening Standard*, 7th February, 1996.

Hatley, R. (1996) 'Steady finger on the trigger.' *The Times*, 2nd October.

LAS (1993) *Report of the Inquiry into the London Ambulance Service*, London: LAS.

Shears, R. (1996) 'If I kept a pet in the condition I'm in, he said, they'd prosecute me. Then he pressed the button.' *Daily Mail*, September 27th, 29.

Shneiderman, B. (1992) *Designing the User Interface*, Reading, MA: Addison–Wesley.

Simpson, A. (1985) *Advanced Techniques in dBase II*, Berkeley.

Urquhart, F. (1996) 'Couple who wooed on the Net are wed.' *The Scotsman*, August.

9.10 Further reading

Norman, D. (1992) *Turn Signals are the Expressions of Automobiles*, Reading, MA: Addison–Wesley 1992.

Norman examines and questions some of the assumptions we make about society and the tools we use. It develops the ideas from his earlier book and looks at how design ignores people.

Norman, D. (1993) *Things That Make Us Smart*, Reading, MA: Addison–Wesley. Norman looks at the relationship between people and the tools they use.

9.11 Electronic resources

Mason's Computer Law Reports, University of Strathclyde
http://law-www-server.law.strath.ac.uk/diglib/mlr.html

Learnability	How easy it is to learn a system.
Likert scale	A scalar questionnaire which uses words to indicate degree.
Las Vegas effect	The garish effect caused by too many colours on the screen.
Long term memory	Storage area of memory.
Luminance	The light reflected from the surface of an object.
Matching	In experiments making sure that the subjects from two groups are the same in background, experience, age, gender etc.
Multi choice questions	Questions where the possible answers are given to the subject and the ones that apply are ticked.
Multi point rating scale	This has a set of values which subjects can select as reflecting their views.
Magic number	George Miller's magic number 7 ± 2 which he suggested was the limit of short term memory.
Null hypothesis	States that the hypothesis will not be true.
Olfaction	The sense of smell.
Open questions	Questions which the subject is free to answer in any way.
Order effect	Biasing the experiment by the order in which tasks are done.
Practice effect	The subject of an experiment improves because of repetition of the task.
Primacy effect	The ability to remember the first few words of a list.
Rapid prototyping	Building examples quickly for fast evaluation with the user.
Recency effect	The ability to remember the last few words of a list.
Repetitive strain injury	Injury caused by repeated movements of the same joints.
Retina	Area of the eye responsible for sight.
Rods	In the eye, receptors sensitive to light.
Saturation	Refers to the extent to which the colour is a chromatic rather than a achromatic colour.
Self administered questionnaires	Questionnaire administered by the subject.
Semantic differential scale	A questionnaire type which asks users to indicate preferences by assigning choices to two opposing descriptions.

Semantic memory	Memory for words.
Sensory memory	The memory of the senses.
Sequence bias	Affecting the subject's responses by the order in which questions are asked.
Short term memory	Area of memory that was believed held ideas for a short time.
Socio-technical design	The process by which design considers the whole working environment.
State transition diagrams	Method of representing the interface which shows possible states of the interface and how they interact with each other.
Static effort	Muscular effort that does not involve movement.
Storyboards	Method of representing screen designs by showing what the interface will look like and how it is linked to the various parts. Storyboards are often made from paper.
Stroop effect	The effect achieved when words conflict with another source of information, such as colours written in the 'wrong' colours.
Taylorism	Dividing tasks into small, discrete actions and having workers perform just one such action, a production line.
Throughput	How easily information is processed or tasks done.
Upright position	This refers to the way in which some VDU users sit at the keyboard with the body held upright.
Usability	How easy it is to learn and use a system.
Usability engineering	The process by which the usability of a system is guaranteed.
Usability metrics	Measurements that can be taken to measure how usable a system is.
Usability specification	A statement about which metrics will apply to a system and what their levels will be.
Visual acuity	The ability to see objects clearly.
Visual field	The range in degrees discernible to the average human being.
Wavelength	The distance apart between each wave crest.
Wizard of Oz	Method by which the design team pretends to be the system and watches user response.
Working memory	Area of memory where conscious thought takes place.

WYSIWYG   'What you see is what you get,' for example in word processing the document looks exactly the same in hard copy as it does on the screen.

Index